A Window on Literature

Literary texts for early and mid-intermediate learners of English

GILLIAN LAZAR

PUBLISHED BY THE PRESS SYNDICATE OF THE UNIVERSITY OF CAMBRIDGE
The Pitt Building, Trumpington Street, Cambridge CB2 1RP, United Kingdom

CAMBRIDGE UNIVERSITY PRESS
The Edinburgh Building, Cambridge CB2 2RU, United Kingdom
40 West 20th Street, New York, NY 10011–4211, USA
10 Stamford Road, Oakleigh, Melbourne 3166, Australia

First published 1999

Printed in the United Kingdom at the University Press, Cambridge

ISBN 0 521 56770 X Book
ISBN 0 521 56769 6 Cassette

Contents

Table of contents

Teachers please note: In some cases there is an overlap between the language focus and literary focus in the texts, since the literary qualities are conveyed through the language.

Unit	Texts	Themes	Language focus	Literary focus
7 Sharing	*The Zoo Story* (play extract) by Edward Albee	Sharing City life	Gaining power in conversation	Understanding character Understanding emotional force of language
8 Memories	*Autobiography* (poem) by Louis MacNeice	Childhood memories Autobiography	Simple past	Interpreting figurative language and paradox
9 Maids and madams	*The Lady's Maid* (short story extract) by Katherine Mansfield *Madam and her Madam* (poem) by Langston Hughes	Loyalty Servants	Past tenses for telling a story	Understanding point of view
10 Music and birdsong	*The Birds Began to Sing* (short story) by Janet Frame	A walk in the countryside Nature versus art	Descriptive language Nature vocabulary Simple past	Understanding figurative language Understanding theme
11 Parents	*The Porch* (play extract) by Jennifer Johnson *A Proud Old Man (Grandpa)* (poem) by Paul Chidyausiku	Ageing	Conversational discourse Pronominal reference	Understanding character Stylistic analysis
12 An excursion	*The Rabbit* (poem) by Alan Brownjohn	Conservation Endangered species	Present and future tenses	Poetic repetition Understanding theme

To the teacher

A Window on Literature is a collection of authentic literary texts designed to be used with teenage and adult learners of English at the early to mid-intermediate level. The texts in the book were chosen not only for their relative linguistic simplicity, but also because they embody themes that should appeal to students from different cultures around the world. The range of texts reflects the rich variety of writing throughout the English-speaking world, both in terms of author and genre. The collection includes poems, extracts from plays, short stories and novels, and one complete short story (Janet Frame's *The Birds Began to Sing*).

Aims of the material

Using literary texts with students at lower levels may seem a daunting task. Firstly, the language of literary texts may appear to be very difficult for learners who are still grappling with elementary grammar and vocabulary. In addition, the texts may refer to cultural beliefs or practices which are alien to the students. Finally, the texts often pose questions about what they mean rather than provide straightforward answers. On the other hand, these very difficulties can make the literary text a valuable source of stimulating and motivating classroom activities. By exposing students to the rich language of the text, we can expand their language awareness, their overall knowledge of how words and grammar can be used. By presenting students with the complex themes in the literary text, we can motivate them to reflect imaginatively on their own experience and on that of writers in different societies. By gently encouraging them to make their own interpretation of a text, we can develop their confidence in forming well-reasoned interpretations of the language that they read and hear.

Format of the material

A Window on Literature consists of twelve units, each based on a different theme. Some of the units include only one literary text, others include two texts linked together by the common theme. There is no specific grading or progression throughout the book, so teachers are free to choose the order in which they use the units.

Teachers may find that a number of different criteria influence their choice of which units to use. Firstly, some of the units have a fairly obvious link with particular grammatical structures or functions, and can be used to consolidate or revise them. For example, the unit entitled 'Do what I say!' (Unit 1) can be used as further practice for imperatives, while 'An excursion' (Unit 12) can be used to consolidate various future tenses. On the other hand, teachers may choose a unit because it touches on particular literary features, for example, 'Maids and madams' (Unit 9) deals with the notion of point of view and 'Memories' (Unit 8) with figurative language. While in these two units there is a fairly *explicit* focus on literary terms and devices, in many units the literary focus is more *implicit*. This is because students at the early to mid-intermediate level need to feel free to experience and enjoy the creative language of literature, without being overloaded by literary metalanguage. With more literary-minded learners teachers can, of course, spell out the literary features of a text more explicitly. Finally, teachers may select a particular unit because its theme fits in well with the syllabus or seems relevant to the interests of a particular group of students.

A summary of the main content of each unit is provided in the table of contents on pages iv–v. This is for teachers to use as a quick guide for selecting which unit is appropriate for their lesson.

Activities in the material

All the activities in the book aim to provide early to mid-intermediate level students with sufficient support and guidance to tackle the texts. Teachers are free to choose which activities will work best with their learners, depending on the degree of support that the learners require. There are a number of different types of activities:

Warm-up activities

These precede the listening to or reading of the text, and are intended to get students thinking about the theme of the unit, or to stimulate their interest in a particular text.

Vocabulary activities

These are designed to help students' comprehension of the vocabulary in the text. In most units, these exercises are deliberately kept short, and definitions of selected words in the text are provided in the panel at the end of the unit. Teachers should encourage students to try to guess the meaning of the words from context while reading, and to use the notes in the panel only after having done so.

Comprehension activities

These follow the listening to or reading of the text, and are generally traditional comprehension questions that focus on the factual meaning of the text. Students at the early to mid-intermediate level often need to feel they have established the 'facts' of the text before they can move on to tasks involving more open-ended interpretation. Answers for these activities are provided in the answer key, and they are marked in this way: 🔑

Activities concerning the language of the text

These tasks focus on the linguistic and literary qualities of the text, for example unusual uses of collocation, figurative language, rhyme, style, etc. Naturally, students at this level cannot be expected to engage in full-blooded analysis of the linguistic and literary qualities of the text, even though many may be highly literate in their own language. However, some attempt is made in each unit to focus on the unusual linguistic features in the text, so that students can gradually acquire the tools for a more sophisticated literary analysis in English. Where appropriate, the answers for tasks of this kind can be found in the answer key.

Activities to encourage inference and interpretation

Despite their limited linguistic resources, students at the earlier stages of learning English are able to engage in complex interpretations of text. However, they may not always have the language to frame their interpretation. Each unit, therefore, includes at least one activity in which students have to make their own interpretation of the text, or draw some inferences about it. Some of these activities are highly structured, offering students a set of interpretations from which to choose. If students are confident about making their own interpretations, teachers may prefer to adapt these activities so that students have greater freedom.

Activities to encourage creative response

Each section of the book concludes with activities that encourage students to speak or write imaginatively. Again, some of these tasks are more structured than others, and teachers may need to adapt them according to the level of guidance required by their students.

The cassette

The accompanying audio-cassette includes all the texts in the book, read in appropriate accents. It can be used with the texts in a number of ways. Firstly, students can listen to the cassette while reading the texts, as suggested in the instructions in most units (this is marked with this sign:). Alternatively, teachers can use the cassette as listening comprehension *before* they read the text, or as consolidation after the text has already been read. Teachers may also like to use the cassette not as listening comprehension per se, but to focus on intonation, mood and interpretation of meaning. This type of intensive listening may be useful in units where students are asked to 'act out' part of a text (e.g. 'Plans and decisions' (Unit 2)).

Notes

The notes at the end of each unit include definitions of some of the words, giving the meaning of the word *as it is used in the text*. The notes also include brief biographical information about the authors of the texts used in the unit, and some notes about the author's style, typical themes, etc. On the whole, the language in these reference notes is pitched slightly higher than the language of the rest of the book. Teachers can, therefore, encourage students to read them with the help of a dictionary. They can be used at the end of the lesson, with students being asked to make the link between the notes and the texts used in the lesson. There may also be instances where teachers prefer to read and discuss the notes with students *before* the texts are read.

1 Do what I say!

Text 1

1 What is a grown-up?
Who usually uses the word 'grown-up'?
Look at these pictures. What do you think a grown-up might say to the children in each picture?

Write the words the grown-up might say:

e.g. Don't feed the dog. ....

....

....

....

....

....

Show your sentences to another student.

2 Now read and listen to the poem *Chivvy*.

Chivvy by **Michael Rosen**

Grown-ups say things like:
Speak up.
Don't talk with your mouth full
Don't stare
Don't point 5
Don't pick your nose
Sit up
Say please
Less noise
Shut the door behind you 10
Don't drag your feet
Haven't you got a hankie?

Take your hands out of your pockets
Pull your socks up
Stand up straight 15
Say thank you
Don't interrupt
No one thinks you're funny
Take your elbows off the table

Can't you make your *own* 20
mind up about anything?

Put a tick next to any sentences in the poem which are like the sentences you wrote in Exercise 1. Tell your partner which ones are the same.

3 Read and listen to the poem again.
Then, can you complete this paragraph about the *last two lines* of the poem?

Grown-ups tell children what to do all the time, and if the children don't listen to them, the grown-ups become cross. But, at the same time, grown-ups also want children to ....

....

....

4 Divide into groups of three or four. One of you pretend to be the grown-up who is speaking in the poem. Read the poem aloud. Think about the *way* you read the poem – for example, are you cross or bored? The others pretend to be the children, who the grown-up is speaking to. Mime the actions. *Remember*: Children, you need to do the actions *before* the grown-up speaks to you!

5 Write down some answers to the following questions, and then discuss them with another student.

How old should children or teenagers be when they make up their own minds about

(a) what subjects to study at school?
(b) what clothes to wear?
(c) what friends to have?
(d) what food to eat?
(e) what job to do when they are older?
(f) where to go without an adult?

Text 2

6 You are going to read another poem. But first look at this definition:

> charity (noun) money or help given to people who are poor, sick, etc.

(a) Do you think that charity is a good or bad thing? Why?
(b) In your country are there any special times when people give to charity? When? What do people give?

7 You are going to read and listen to a poem called *Feeding the Poor at Christmas* by Eunice de Souza, a writer from Goa in India. From the title of the poem can you guess

(a) who gets the charity?
(b) what do they get?
(c) when do they get it?

Now read and listen to the poem.

Feeding the Poor at Christmas by **Eunice de Souza**

Every Christmas we feed the poor.
We arrive an hour late: Poor dears,
Like children waiting for a treat.
Bring your plates. Don't move.
Don't try turning up for more. 5
No. Even if you don't drink
you can't take your share
for your husband. Say thank you
and a rosary for us every evening.

No. Not a towel and a shirt, 10
even if they're old.
What's that you said?
You're a good man, Robert, yes,
beggars can't be, exactly.

8 In the poem, we hear the words of the speaker, a person who is helping to feed the poor at Christmas. But we don't hear the poor people to whom the speaker is talking. Here are a few ideas about what the poor people in the poem say to the speaker:

(a) Can I have another place of rice?
Don't try turning up for more.

(b) Could I give it to my husband instead?
....

(c) May I please have these two things?
....

(d) Well, beggars can't be choosers I suppose.
....

Read and listen to the poem again, and see if you can find the answers that the speaker gives to these words. The first one has been done for you.

9 'Beggars can't be choosers.' What does this expression mean in English? Complete the following definition:

Poor people must take .... they can get, and must not hope to

.... exactly what they ....

Do you agree with this expression? Why?

10 Do you agree with the following sentences about the poem? Discuss them with another student.

The people who feed the poor at Christmas

- are very kind and generous
- think that they are better than poor people
- don't show any respect for poor people
- like telling poor people what to do
- show a lot of love for poor people
- think that poor people are like small children

Can you write your own sentence about the *poor people* in the poem? Talk to other students about your sentence.

11 In both *Chivvy* and *Feeding the Poor at Christmas* there are a lot of *orders* (a phrase or sentence where one person tells somebody to do something). Can you fill in this table about both the poems?

	Chivvy	*Feeding the Poor at Christmas*
Some orders in the poem	*Speak up*	
Who gives the order		
Who the order is for		

What kind of relationship is there between the person who gives the order, and the person who has to listen to it?

Can you think of other relationships where one person may use a lot of orders when they speak to the other person?

Creative development

Do one of the following exercises (or both if you have time).

(a) Look at the following dialogue:

CHILD	Rob is pulling my hair, Miss.
TEACHER	Stop that, now, Rob!
CHILD	I left my book at home, Miss.
TEACHER	Again? I'm really getting tired of this!
CHILDREN	Can't we go now, Miss?
TEACHER	Another five minutes.
CHILDREN	....
TEACHER	I said another five minutes!
CHILDREN	Now, Miss?
TEACHER	....
CHILDREN	....
TEACHER	....
CHILDREN	....
TEACHER	....

Can you fill in the missing words of the dialogue between the children and the teacher?

Then choose either the words of the children or the words of the teacher. Use these words as a poem. Think of a title for this poem. Practise reading it out aloud to the other students in your class!

(b) Think of a relationship where two people are not equal, and the one gives orders to the other. Write the words of the person who gives all the orders. Read these words aloud to the other students in your class. Do NOT tell them who the speaker is. Can they guess?

NOTES

Chivvy

Vocabulary

chivvy: ask somebody again and again to do something that they do not want to do

stare (line 4): look at somebody for a long time

point (line 5): hold your finger out to show somebody or something

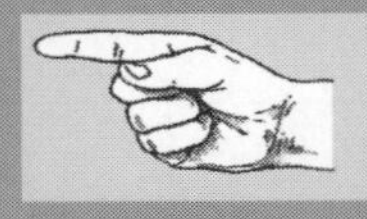

drag your feet (line 11): walk slowly without lifting your feet

hankie (line 12): handkerchief; a square piece of cloth you use for blowing your nose

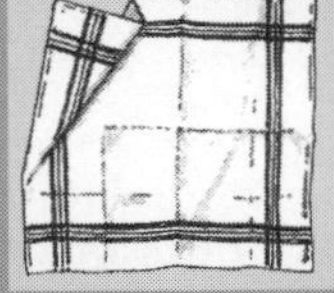

interrupt (line 17): say something when somebody is already talking

elbow (line 19): the middle part of your arm where it bends

make your own mind up about something (lines 20–21): decide what you think about something

Michael Rosen (1946–)

British poet and performer. Educated at Oxford University and the National Film School, Rosen's first book of poetry for children *Mind your own Business* was published in 1974. Since then he has written many books of poetry for children, including *Don't put Mustard in the Custard* (1984), and has edited many collections of poems for children.

Rosen is interested not only in the meaning of words, but also their grammar and sounds. His poems use playful spoken language to explore ordinary life in a fresh way.

Feeding the Poor at Christmas

Vocabulary

treat (line 3): something special that you give somebody or do for them because you know they will enjoy it

rosary (line 9): a prayer in the Catholic religion

beggar (line 14): a person who lives by asking people in the street for food or money

Eunice de Souza (1940–)

Indian poet and art critic. Born in Goa, which was once a Portuguese colony, de Souza was educated at the University of Bombay and in the United States. She has written three books of poetry, including *Ways of Belonging* (1990), children's tales and articles on art.

De Souza's poetry deals with the different European and Indian traditions of Goan society, including the Catholic religion. Her poems are short and exact, and many describe the anger and violence of women's lives.

2 Plans and decisions

1 What are your hopes and plans for the future? Make some sentences about your life, using the table below to help you.

In the next month Next summer In the next two years In five years time In ten years time	I hope to ..... I plan to ..... I want to .....

Tell your hopes and plans to another student. Are any of your hopes and plans the same?

2 Now read and listen to the following text, and finish these sentences:

(a) Peter plans to ....

(b) His mother wants him to ....

(c) His father wants him to ....

from *To Be A Farmer's Boy* by **C. P. Taylor**

Part 1

PETER	Mum ... I want to talk to you about the farm ... I know you want me to stay on at school ...	
MUM	Do what the hell you like ...	
PETER	Dad wants me to take the job, too, Mum ...	
MUM	I've given up ... I told you ... It's finished ... There's nothing I can do about it ...	5
PETER	Yes ... That's the best way, Mum ...	
MUM	What do you mean it's the best way? ... What do you know about anything ... You're just a child ... Just lie down and die ... Is that the best way to live? ... You want to be a teacher ... They said at the school ... You had it in you ... You could be a teacher ... you could maybe even get to a university ...	10
PETER	Mother ... It's alright ... If I can't be a teacher ... I'm not worried ...	
MUM	You know that ... I don't want you to be a damn *farmer* ... I want you to better yourself, I've had farms enough with your father ... That's enough to put up with for half a *dozen* lifetimes ...	
PETER	I'll be getting a pound a week ... and my keep ...	15
MUM	What are you *doing* to me, Peter ...	
PETER	I'm talking to you about going to Briar Farm ...	
MUM	You're *not* talking to me ... That's *not* talking to me ... What are you *talking* about? ...	
PETER	Mum ... I want to ... I really want to go, Mum ... *Look* at me ...	
MUM	I can't bear looking at you, just now ...	20
PETER	*Look* at me ... (*THRUSTS HIS FACE IN FRONT OF HERS*)	

3 Match these expressions from the text with the correct definitions:

(1) to give up (line 5)	(a) to improve your position in society
(2) to have it in you (line 9)	(b) to stop doing something
(3) to better yourself (lines 12–13)	(c) to have the ability to do something
(4) to put up with (lines 13–14)	(d) to accept something that is hard or unpleasant

4 Here are some sentences about the text. Can you write down which line in the text has the same meaning as each sentence? The first one has been done for you.

(a) Peter and his father agree with each other. (line .4.)
(b) Peter's mum says she can't change his dad's ideas or Peter's ideas. (line ...)

(c) Peter has the ability to continue his studies and get a good job. (line ...)
(d) Peter's mother has found her life as the wife of a farmer very difficult. (line ...)
(e) If Peter takes the farm job, the farmer will give him food, a place to live and four pounds a month. (line ...)

5 Pretend you are Peter. What does he say to his mother next? Write down your ideas. Then read and listen to the next part of the play.

Part 2

MUM	You're a proper devil ... You are ... the oldest and the worst ...	
PETER	I know ... I am ...	
MUM	Why do you say that, boy? ...	
PETER	BECAUSE I am ... It's the truth ...	25
MUM	You're not ... That was just my temper ...	
PETER	I am ...	
MUM	Peter ... Come here, child ... I didn't mean that ...	
PETER	Look at me a minute ... Mum ...	
MUM	What's there to see ... Looking at *you*? ...	30
PETER	Look at me ...	
MUM	What's the *matter* with you, boy? ...	
PETER	It's alright ... Can't you see, Mum ... I'm happy ... Look at me ...	
MUM	*I'm* not ...	
PETER	*I* am ...	35
MUM	What's happened ... then ... You're happy ...	
PETER	I'm always happy ... Most of the time ... I'm a happy character ... aren't I ...	
MUM	You're sort of ... I am, too ... when I'm not miserable ... I could be a very happy person ...	
PETER	You know that ... It'll be better for everybody ... If I take this job, Mum ... I'm fourteen ... We've no money ... It's one less to feed ... and I can bring some money home ...	40
MUM	*Oh!*	
PETER	What do you, mean 'Oh' ...	
MUM	I'm not having that ... I'm not having people sacrificing themselves like that ... I don't believe in it ... I know that ... Sacrificing yourself like that doesn't do anybody any good ... You're staying on another year at school ... You *hear* me ...	45

6 True or False?

(a) Peter's mum wants to be left alone.
(b) Peter's mum says that he causes a lot of problems.
(c) Peter's mum is not sorry that she lost her temper.
(d) Peter can help his family by giving them some of his money.
(e) Peter's mother says she will let him work at Briar Farm.

7 Peter and his mother have very strong feelings that show in the *way* they speak to each other. Look at these four examples of his mother's words:

(a) 'Do what the hell you like ...' (line 3)
(b) 'I've given up ... I told you ... It's finished ... There's nothing I can do about it' (line 5)
(c) 'Peter ... Come here, child ... I didn't mean that ...' (line 28)
(d) 'I'm not having that ... I'm not having people sacrificing themselves like that ...' (line 45)

In what *way* does Peter's mother say these words? How does she *feel* when she says them? Choose from this list of ideas:

- She speaks *angrily* (she feels angry)
- She speaks in a *determined* way (she feels strongly that what she wants should happen)
- She speaks in a *resigned* way (she feels she can't change anything, and has to stop complaining)
- She speaks *kindly* (she wants to make Peter feel better)

Read and listen to the texts again. Can you find other examples where Peter or his mother speak angrily or kindly, or in a resigned or determined way? What other feelings do they have while they are speaking?

8 Look at these six paragraphs about Peter and his mum.

(a) Peter is a young and loving son who really wants to help his family. He doesn't listen to what his mother says only because he wants to help her.
(b) Peter's mum is a passive person who will never be happy about anything.
(c) Peter is a foolish teenager who doesn't think carefully about his future. He is afraid to disagree with his father.
(d) Peter's mum is a loving mother, who really wants her son to have a better life than she has.
(e) Peter is a strong person who really wants to be free of his family and live how he wants.
(f) Peter's mum is an angry and difficult woman who is not practical about life.

Write a number next to each paragraph:

1 I don't agree
2 This is partly true
3 I completely agree

Explain your reasons to the other students in your class.

9 In pairs pretend that one of you is Peter, and one of you is his mum.

If you like, listen to the first part of the tape again. Pay attention to the *feeling* in the voices of Peter and his mother. Which words do they stress while they speak?

(a) Read the text aloud from line 1 to line 21.
(b) Read the text again from line 1 to line 21, but this time make sure you have a lot of *feeling* in your voice – be angry or kind, determined or resigned.
(c) If you can, stand up and read the text again. This time use your hands and move around a bit.
(d) Now try to act out the scene between Peter and his mother, but this time without looking at the text. You don't need to use the same words as the text.

10 Should Peter stay at school OR should Peter leave school and take the job at Briar Farm?
What do you think? Why? Write down at least *three* reasons for your ideas. Then find somebody in your class who does *not* agree with you. Tell them your reasons. Listen to their reasons. Do you still think you are right?

Does this kind of problem happen in your country? Talk to other students about it.

Creative development

Complete the following
In the next year, I need to decide whether

(a) .... OR

(b) ....

Reasons to do (a)	*Reasons to do (b)*

Then talk about your decision with another student. What does he or she think you should do? What do *you* think you should do? Why?

NOTES

To be a Farmer's Boy

Vocabulary

Part 1

what the hell (line 3), *damn* (line 12): these words are used to stress how strongly you feel about something; they are used in informal, spoken English and some people think they are rude

dozen (line 14): twelve

keep (line 15): food and a place to live

I can't bear looking at you (line 20): I'm too cross or upset to look at you (we usually say 'I can't bear *to do* something')

Part 2

a proper devil (line 22): a person who causes many problems

temper (line 26): a state in which you get angry very suddenly

miserable (line 38): very unhappy

sacrificing (line 45): giving up something important to help someone else

C. P. Taylor (1929–1981)

British playwright. Born in Scotland, C. P. Taylor spent most of his life in the north-east of England. He wrote more than seventy plays – for television and radio as well as for community theatre and his local village. His best known play *Good* was produced by the Royal Shakespeare Company.

C. P. Taylor was interested in people, their relationships to each other and the society they live in. His plays are full of warm humour, and use small realistic details to explore important themes.

3 Fairy stories

Text 1

1 What is a fairy story or a fairy tale? Do you know any names of fairy stories in English?

2 Look at these pictures of some of the real or imaginary people and animals we sometimes find in fairy tales. Can you label them using these words:

witch dragon giant fairy prince princess

3 Can you add to these lists?

Objects/things we sometimes find in fairy tales ....

....

Places we sometimes find in fairy tales ....

....

4 **Can you complete these sentences about a typical fairy story in English?**

The hero (e.g. the youngest son of a poor man) has to leave home. He meets a person or creature (e.g. ....) who gives him an object that is magic (e.g. ....). With the magic object, he does something really difficult (e.g. ....). He has shown that he is clever or ...., and so for his reward he ....

Are there any fairy stories like this in your own language? How are they different from this one?

5 **Read and listen to this poem.**

Fairy Story by **Stevie Smith**

I went into the wood one day
And there I walked and lost my way

When it was so dark I could not see
A little creature came to me

He said if I would sing a song 5
The time would not be very long

But first I must let him hold my hand tight
Or else the wood would give me a fright

I sang a song, he let me go
But now I am home again there is nobody I know. 10

Think about these questions:

(a) Are any of the people, creatures, things or places in your lists (Exercise 3) in the poem? If so, which ones?

(b) In what way is the poem like the typical fairy story in Exercise 4? In what way is it different?

6 **In fairy stories, the hero or heroine often changes in some way. Read or listen to the poem again. How do you think that the speaker changed by meeting the creature in the wood? Talk to other students about your ideas.**

7 We asked people to give us their ideas about the poem. Here are some of them:

I don't like it – it is a bit frightening.

Strange, but not really like a fairy story because there is no happy ending.

It seems very simple and easy to read, but I think it describes somebody's lonely feelings.

It has a simple rhyme like a song for children, but I think its meaning is too frightening for children.

Which ideas do you agree with? Why?

What do you think the poem means?

Write your own sentences about the poem. Read them to the other students in your class. Do they agree or disagree with you?

Text 2

8 Can you draw this? Use a dictionary to help you.

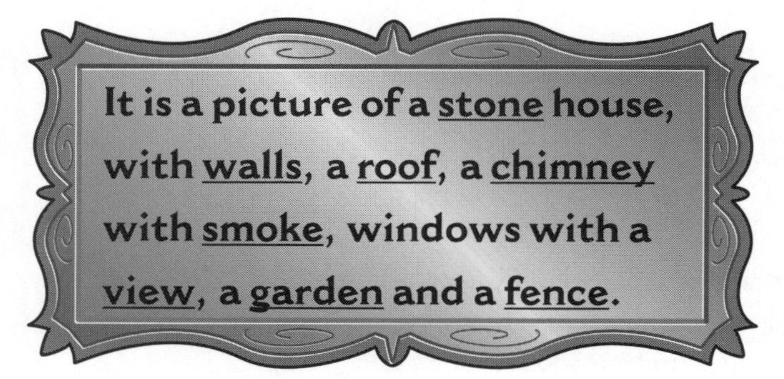

Pin your drawing up in your classroom, or show your drawing to other students.

9 What does a house mean to you? A place to be safe? A place to find peace? A worry because you have to clean it? And what does a garden mean to you?

Can you complete these two sentences?

For me, a house means ....

For me, a garden means ....

Compare your ideas with another student. Are they the same or different?

10 Read and listen to this poem.

Fairy Tale by **Miroslav Holub**

He built himself a house,
his foundations,
his stones,
his walls,
his roof overhead, 5
his chimney and smoke,
his view from the window.

He made himself a garden,
his fence,
his thyme, 10
his earthworm,
his evening dew.

He cut out his bit of sky above.

And he wrapped the garden in the sky
and the house in the garden 15
and packed the lot in a handkerchief

and went off
lone as an arctic fox
through the cold
unending 20
rain
into the world.

(translated from Czech by **George Theiner**)

---

11 For the poet, what do you think the house and the garden mean?

12 Read and listen to the poem again. Then use a dictionary to help you fill in this table:

The way we usually use the word	*In the poem*
What do we usually 'cut out'? a picture/photo/article in the newspaper a dress if you are sewing	line 13: his bit of sky
What do we usually 'wrap'?	lines 14–15
What do we usually 'pack'?	line 16:

13 What is unusual about the way the words 'cut out', 'wrap' and 'pack' are used in lines 13–16? What effect does this have?

14 Here are some ideas about the meanings or themes of the poem. Tick the one(s) you like the most. Write your own ideas, and talk to another student about them.

- Life is lonely.
- You can only trust yourself.
- Material things are not important.
- ....
- ....

15 Which poem do you prefer – *Fairy Story* or *Fairy Tale*? Why?
Do you think the titles *Fairy Story* and *Fairy Tale* are the right ones for each poem? Why?

Creative development

Here are three *beginnings* for a fairy story:

Once upon a time, there was

- a king who had three beautiful daughters.
- a poor woodcutter with three sons.
- a very rich man who was very unhappy.

And here are three *endings*:

And so,

- the princess and the young man lived happily ever after.
- they had a great feast and lived happily ever after.
- the woodcutter and his family were never hungry again, and lived happily ever after.

Work by yourself, or in pairs or groups with other students. Choose one of the beginnings and/or one of the endings, and write the middle part of the story.
In your story will there be a dragon? A princess? A giant? A poisoned apple? A tower? Or none of them at all?
Will your story be like a typical fairy story, or will it be like one of the poems in this unit?

Read your stories aloud to your class.

NOTES

Fairy Story

Vocabulary

I lost my way (line 2): I didn't know where I was

creature (line 4): a strange or imaginary living thing

wood (line 8): an area of land covered with trees

Stevie Smith (1902–1971)

British poet and novelist. She lived in her aunt's house in London from the age of three until she died, and worked as a secretary for the same publishing house for thirty years. She wrote three novels and eight books of poetry. The best known is *Not Waving but Drowning* (1957).

Her poems are witty, but also strange and unexpected. Although they are written in the language we use every day, they are full of strong images. They deal with relationships, loneliness, love and death.

Fairy Tale

Vocabulary

foundations (line 2): the strong base in the earth on which you build something

thyme (line 10): a plant or herb which is used to make food more tasty

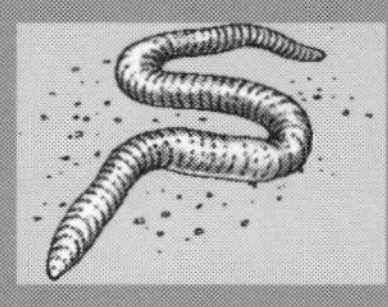

earthworm (line 11): a long thin animal with no legs or backbone that lives in the earth

dew (line 12): small drops of water that appear on the ground at night

lone (line 18): without any other person

arctic (line 18): coming from the most northern part of the world, which is very cold

Miroslav Holub (1923– 1998)

Czech writer. Trained as an immunologist (a scientist who studies how the body reacts to illness), Holub wrote 14 books of poetry, five collections of prose and many scientific papers.

His poems often describe the beauty and mystery of what the scientist sees through a microscope. He believed the language of poetry should be clear, based on facts and understood by everyone. He used ideas from classical writers (like Homer) and traditional Czech stories in his writing.

4 An empty room

1 Imagine you are looking for a room to rent and live in. Here are some things that are important when you look for this room:

- SIZE (how big or small is the room?)
- LIGHT (does it get good light?)
- NOISE (is the room noisy or quiet?)
- VIEW (is there a good view out the windows?)
- AREA (where is the room, and what is it near?)
- AGE (is it old or modern?)
- COLOUR OF WALLS
- WARMTH (is the room cold or warm?)
- PRICE (how much does it cost?)

Decide which are the *three* most important things on the list for you. Talk to other students about them, and give reasons for your choice.

2 You are going to read and listen to the beginning of a play called *Here* by Michael Frayn. Here is a description of the room on the stage in which the play happens. Use a dictionary to help you understand the description of the room.

> *An empty room.*
> *Two doors. Window. Bare floor, bare walls, no furniture. A kitchenette cupboard, shelves, and an alcove with a curtain, now pulled back to reveal a rail with a few wire coat-hangers on it.*

Decide which of these drawings of the room match the description above.

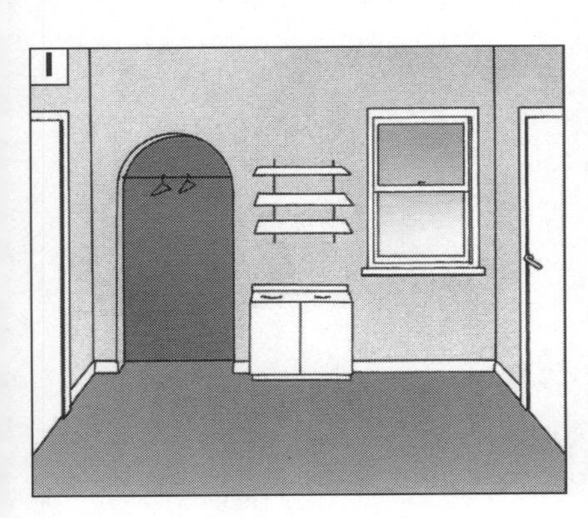

3 Now imagine that two people come to look at the room to decide if they want to rent it. Who might rent a room of this kind? A family? Students? Two friends? Write down your ideas. Then read and listen to the text.

---

from *Here* by **Michael Frayn**

One of the doors is unlocked and pushed open. On the threshold stands CATH, *holding the key on a label. She comes cautiously into the room, followed by* PHIL. *They look dubiously around.*

CATH No?

PHIL No. No? 5

CATH No.

PHIL *goes out.* CATH *takes a last look round. He reappears.*

PHIL What?

CATH Nothing.

They both look round. 10

PHIL You mean ... ?

CATH No ... No!

She goes out. He continues to look around the room.

PHIL No.

He turns to go. She reappears. 15

CATH Not unless you ... ?

PHIL Me? No. Not if you ... ?

CATH No ...

She looks round the room.

PHIL I mean, what do you think? 20

CATH I don't know ...

PHIL Oh, I see.

CATH No, no – if you think no ...

PHIL Yes, but I want to know what *you* think.

CATH I think you think no. 25

PHIL You mean you *don't* think no?

CATH I just think ... I don't know ...

PHIL You don't think *yes*? You're not saying you think *yes*?

CATH No! No.

PHIL	But you don't think no?	30
CATH	No, but I know *you* think no.	
PHIL	Not at all.	
CATH	You *don't* think no?	
PHIL	Not if *you* don't think no.	
CATH	No, well ...	35
	They move about the room, looking. She opens the kitchenette.	
PHIL	What?	
CATH	The cooker's a bit ...	
PHIL	Yes.	
	She closes it. He opens the second door.	40
	So's the bath.	
	She looks as well.	
CATH	Yes ...	
	He closes it. She pulls the curtain across to close off the alcove.	
	Not very ...	45
PHIL	Not very.	
	She draws the curtain back again. He looks out of the window.	
CATH	What?	
PHIL	Nothing.	
CATH	The view?	50
	She joins him at the window. They look out.	
	Well ...	
PHIL	Fine.	
CATH	Reasonably.	
PHIL	Absolutely.	55
CATH	Isn't it?	
PHIL	Yes. Yes!	

4 Who are Cath and Phil? Do they like the room to rent? Why? Do you think that they will rent it or not? Why?

5 Cath and Phil often do not finish their sentences in the play, and we have to guess what they mean. Here are two parts of the dialogue from the play again. In groups, can you finish Cath and Phil's sentences for them? Are your ideas the same as other groups?

A

PHIL	What?	
CATH	Nothing	
	They both look round.	10
PHIL	You mean ... ? we should rent/take it?	
CATH	No ... No!	
	She goes out. He continues to look around the room.	
PHIL	No.	
	He turns to go. She reappears.	15
CATH	Not unless you .... ?	
PHIL	Me? No. Not if you	
CATH	No	

B

PHIL	What?	
CATH	The cooker's a bit	
PHIL	Yes.	
	She closes it. He opens the second door.	40
	So's the bath.	
	She looks as well.	
CATH	Yes	
	He closes it. She pulls the curtain across to close off the alcove.	
	Not very	45
PHIL	Not very.	

6 Read and listen to the text again.
Then look at these sentences about the play. Choose one of each pair that you think is true. Explain why you have chosen these sentences to another student.

(a) Cath and Phil are very close to each other.
(b) Cath and Phil are too close to each other.

(c) Cath and Phil decide about things easily.
(d) Cath and Phil cannot decide easily.

(e) Cath is the stronger person of the two of them.
(f) Phil is the stronger person of the two of them.

Write one or more sentences about Cath and Phil. Show your sentence to other students. Do they agree with your sentence?

7 Think of the word 'No'. Practise saying this word in as many different ways as you can, for example in an angry way, as a question, in a way that shows you are not sure, etc. How many different ways can you find?

In pairs, decide who is Cath and who is Phil. Practise reading lines 4–14 aloud in pairs. Then, if there is space in your classroom, act these lines out for other students.

8 Imagine that Cath and Phil decide to rent the room. Can you write their dialogue? Use this outline:

CATH ....

PHIL ....

CATH ....

PHIL ....

CATH ....

Try to use the word 'Yes' as many times as you can in the dialogue! Then, read your dialogue aloud to the other students in your class.

Creative development

Do one of the following exercises (or both if you have time).

(a) Imagine you are one of the following:

a writer or musician
a business executive
a student
somebody else you would really like to be

Do not tell any other student about who you are!
Imagine you have rented the empty room that Cath and Phil looked around. It has no furniture, and nothing on the walls or floor. Can you make this room a place where *you* (the new you!) can feel happy and comfortable?

Think about:

- what *colours* you would use in the room
- what kind of *furniture* you would like
- what you would do with the *walls* and the *floor* of the room
- what you would do with the *window* of the room
- what *other things* (e.g. books, plants, etc.) you would put in the room

Draw a plan of your room. Explain your plan to another student, without saying *who* you are. Can they *guess* who you are? How?

(b) Read and listen to the text again. Then divide into pairs. One of you take the part of Cath, and one of you take the part of Phil. Read the whole text aloud. If you have enough space in your classroom, move about and act out the text as you read.
What happens next? Act out your ideas.

NOTES

Vocabulary

on the threshold (line 1): on the area of floor at the entrance to a room or building

cautiously (line 2): carefully

dubiously (line 3): in a way that shows you are not sure if something will be good or not

reappears (line 7): appears again

draws the curtain (line 47): closes the curtain

reasonably (line 54): okay or good enough, but not completely right

absolutely (line 55): completely right

Michael Frayn (1933–)

English playwright, novelist and journalist. Born in London, Frayn began his career as a journalist, and wrote witty columns for newspapers. He has published many novels, a book about philosophy, and many plays for stage and television. He has also translated some of the plays of Chekhov, the Russian playwright.

Frayn's plays are comedies which make us think about how people behave. He uses humour to laugh gently at his characters. He is good at creating dialogue which seems natural and taken from real life, but which also contains many jokes.

5 Mystery

Text 1

1 What do these words mean?

> 'You can't understand everything. It would be a dull old world if you could.'

Can you understand these happenings? Can you explain them?

(a) A woman looks out of her window one night, and sees something that is round, white and shining. It is moving through the sky very fast.
(b) You are thinking about a friend you saw two years ago. Then the phone rings. It is your friend.
(c) A man can usually tell what the weather will be like next week. He does this by watching his dog.

Has anything strange ever happened to you? Tell the other students in your class about it. Can they explain it?

2 You are going to read and listen to part of a story. The story is called *The Sunflowers in the Snow*.

Can you give some reasons for this strange happening? For example:

- Perhaps the flowers were not real, but were made of plastic.
- ....
- ....

3 Read and listen to the text.

from *The Sunflowers in the Snow* by **William Trevor**

Once upon a time a really fantastic thing happened. In a town in Ireland some sunflowers bloomed in December.

It was a few days before Christmas and there were four inches of snow on the ground. 'The sunflowers imagine it's August', said the people of the town. They didn't know what to think. 5

'Well?' said Dom, a red-haired boy, to Mr Cranley, the butcher.

'I haven't seen them yet,' said Mr Cranley. 'I'll go up one of these days.'

Dom wondered about that. He wondered about Mr Cranley, for he knew that Mr Cranley must know more than most people about the sunflowers. Mr Cranley placed his two hands on his butcher's block 10 and looked down at Dom. He said:

'You can't understand everything, Dom. It would be a dull old world if you could.'

Mr Cranley was the only person in the small town that Dom had ever told his favourite secret to. One day, a year or so ago, he had explained to 15 Mr Cranley about how he used to look out of his bedroom window, watching the people and the seagulls.

Sometimes Mr McCarthy the ironmonger would pass by, taking his dog Bonzo for a walk on a lead, and when that happened Dom would quickly close his eyes and see everything differently. What he saw was 20 Bonzo taking Mr McCarthy for a walk on a lead, and this always made Dom laugh and laugh.

Sometimes when he looked across the street and saw old Mrs Twing feeding the sparrows on her window-sill, Dom would close his eyes and see the sparrows feeding old Mrs Twing. And when Danny Fowler, the 25 milkman, drove up the street with his horse and cart, Dom would close his eyes and see Danny Fowler dragging the cart, while Trot, the horse, delivered the milk bottles. That made Dom laugh so much that his mother would shout up to him to stop at once or there'd be trouble. His mother used to say it was his red hair that made him so excitable. 30

When Dom told Mr Cranley all that, Mr Cranley said: 'You have a Special Gift, Dom. Like someone might have a Special Gift and be able to play beautiful music on a piano or a violin. Or be able to run faster than anyone else. Nobody understands why some people can do things and other people can't.' 35

'Have you a Special Gift, Mr Cranley?' Dom asked.

Mr Cranley didn't reply to that question.

4 Match these words from the text with the pictures below:

(a) *butcher's block (lines 10)* (b) *lead (line 21)*
(c) *seagull (line 17)* (d) *sparrow (line 24)*

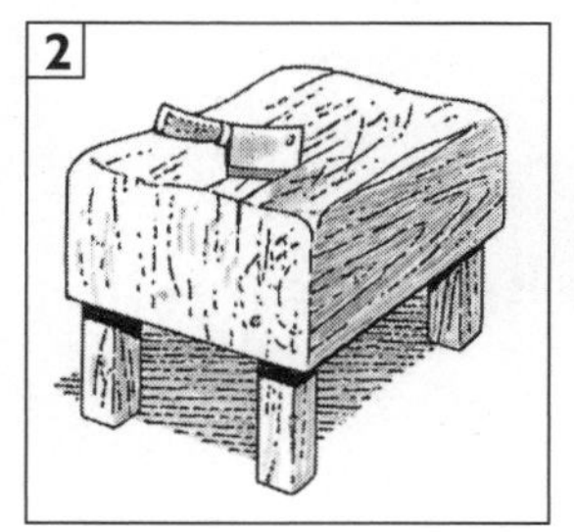

5 Here is a summary of the text you have just read. Some of the summary is not correct. Can you find the wrong information, and write the correct information instead?

Last year, in a ~~city~~ town in ~~Scotland~~ Ireland some sunflowers bloomed in December. The people of the town were not surprised. Dom, a brown-haired boy who lived in the town, wanted to know what Mr Cranley, the doctor, thought about the sunflowers. Mr Cranley and his wife knew Dom's favourite secret, which often made Dom laugh. Dom used to watch people and animals out of his sitting room window. He imagined that the people were animals, and that the animals behaved like people. For example, he imagined a dog called Rover taking his owner for a walk on a lead. Dom told Mr Cranley all about this, and Mr Cranley said that he had a Special Gift. But when Dom asked Mr Cranley if he had a Special Gift, Mr Cranley became very angry.

Now read and listen to the tape again to check that you have written the correct information.

6 In pairs or groups talk about WHY

- the sunflowers bloomed in the snow
- Dom wondered about Mr Cranley and the sunflowers
- Mr Cranley told Dom he couldn't understand everything
- Dom told Mr Cranley his favourite secret
- Mr Cranley told Dom he had a Special Gift
- Mr Cranley didn't answer when Dom asked if he had a Special Gift

What do you think is going to happen next in the story? Write down a few key words or phrases to remind you of your ideas.
Then, tell other students your ideas.
Finally, look at the key in the back of the book. Are your ideas the same as or different from what happens in the story?

7 Do you have any 'Special Gifts'?
Do you know anyone with a 'Special Gift'? What is this gift? Is it a good or bad thing to have a special gift? Why?

Text 2

8 The next extract does not take place in winter, but in a garden on a beautiful summer's day in England. Something strange happens. What is it? Write down your ideas.
Tell your classmates about them.

9 Read and listen to the following text. Edward and Flora are sitting in their large garden on a summer's day. What happens?

---

from *A Slight Ache* by **Harold Pinter**

EDWARD: Ah, it's a good day. I feel it in my bones. In my muscles. I think I'll stretch my legs in a minute. Down to the pool. My God, look at that flowering shrub over there. Clematis. What a wonderful ...
(*He stops suddenly.*)

FLORA: What? 5

(*Pause.*)

Edward, what is it?

(*Pause.*)

Edward ...

EDWARD: (*thickly*) He's there. 10

FLORA: Who?

EDWARD: (*low murmuring*) Blast and damn it, he's there, he's there at the back gate.

FLORA: Let me see.

She moves over to him to look. Pause.

(*Lightly.*) Oh, it's the matchseller. 15

EDWARD He's back again.

FLORA But he's always there.

EDWARD Why? What is he doing there?

FLORA But he's never disturbed you, has he? The man's been standing there for weeks. You've never mentioned it. 20

EDWARD What is he doing there?

FLORA He's selling matches, of course.

EDWARD It's ridiculous. What's the time?

FLORA Half past nine.

EDWARD What in God's name is he doing with a tray full of matches at half past nine in the morning? 25

FLORA He arrives at seven o'clock.

EDWARD Seven o'clock?

FLORA He's always there at seven.

EDWARD Yes, but you've never ... actually seen him arrive? 30

FLORA No, I ...

EDWARD Well, how do you know he's ... not been standing there all night?

(*Pause.*)

FLORA Do you find him interesting, Edward? 35

EDWARD (*casually*) Interesting? No. No, I ... don't find him interesting.

FLORA He's a very nice old man, really.

EDWARD You've spoken to him?

FLORA No. No. I haven't spoken to him. I've nodded.

EDWARD (*pacing up and down*) For two months he's been standing on that spot, do you realize that? Two months. I haven't been able to step outside the back gate. 40

FLORA Why on earth not?

EDWARD (*to himself*) It used to give me great pleasure, such pleasure, to stroll along through the long grass, out through the back gate, pass into the lane. That pleasure is now denied me. It's my own house, isn't it? It's my own gate. 45

FLORA I really can't understand this, Edward.

10 Choose (a) or (b) to explain the meaning of these words in the texts:

(i) '*I feel it in my bones*' (line 1)
You say this when you have
(a) a strong feeling about something
(b) a bad pain

(ii) '*I'll stretch my legs*' (line 2)
You say this when
(a) you are going for a walk
(b) you are going to do some exercises

(iii) *thickly* (line 10)
If you say something thickly, you
(a) sound very tired
(b) are not very clear

(iv) *casually* (line 36)
If you say something casually, you
(a) don't show much interest
(b) are very interested in it

(v) '*That pleasure is now denied me*' (line 45–6) means
(a) you really enjoy something
(b) you are not allowed or able to enjoy something any more

11 Is there anything strange about what happens in the text you have just read? Read and listen to the text again and write down your ideas.

(e.g.) It is strange to find a matchseller in modern England.

....

....

....

....

12 What do Flora and Edward seem to feel about the matchseller? Fill in one of their names in the following sentences:

I think that .... is cross and annoyed with the matchseller.

I think that .... is upset by the matchseller.

I think that .... is interested in the matchseller.

I think that .... is frightened of the matchseller.

I think that .... is kind about the matchseller and warm towards him.

I think that .... isn't worried by the matchseller.

13 Discuss with other students:

- Who is the matchseller?
- Why is he standing at the back gate?
- What is going to happen next in the play?

14 Look at the notes about Pinter on page 34. Read the description of his plays given in the second paragraph. Is this description true of the extract from *A Slight Ache*?
Do you like the extract? Why? Or do you prefer the extract from *The Sunflowers in the Snow*? If so, why?

Creative development

Here are some newspaper headlines and articles about strange happenings:

OLD LADY GETS CARD FROM DEAD FRIEND

A postman yesterday delivered a birthday card to Mrs Edith Stubbs, aged 82. The card, freshly signed, was from her friend Mabel who died ten years ago

Twin brothers win £10,000 each

Two twin brothers, aged forty-eight years old, have not seen each other for thirty years. Today they both won £10,000 each in a competition

Think of a strange happening. Write the headline and the beginning of a newspaper article about. Read it aloud to your class.

NOTES

The Sunflowers in the Snow

Vocabulary

fantastic (line 1): very strange or unreal

bloomed (line 2): grew flowers (used of a tree or plant)

wondered about (line 8): wanted to know more about

placed (line 10): put with care

ironmonger (line 18): a person who sells tools and equipment for your home and garden

dragging (line 27): pulling something heavy

excitable (line 30): if you are excitable then you get excited very easily

gift (line 32): a natural talent or ability

William Trevor (1928–)

Anglo-Irish novelist and short story writer. Born and educated in Ireland, Trevor first became a teacher and a sculptor. His first novel was published in 1958, and since then he has written many novels and collections of short stories, including *Fools of Fortune* (1983) and *Collected Stories* (1992).

Trevor's novels and short stories usually take place in England and Ireland. He writes with humour and sympathy about people who are old, lonely or mad and who live in quite old-fashioned societies. His more recent work deals with the violence of Northern Ireland.

A Slight Ache

Vocabulary

muscle (line 1): one of the parts inside your body, for example in your arms or legs, that you use when you move

shrub (line 3): a low plant with many woody branches, grown in gardens and parks

clematis (line 3): a climbing plant with white, yellow or pink flowers

murmuring (line 12): saying something in a soft low voice that is difficult to understand

matchseller (line 15): a person who, many years ago, used to sell matches in the street

disturbed (line 19): worried, bothered

ridiculous (line 23): very silly

I've nodded (line 39): I've said hello by moving my head up and down

pacing up and down (line 40): walking up and down in a nervous way

pleasure (line 44): a feeling of happiness that comes from something that you enjoy

Harold Pinter (1930–)

British playwright. Born into a working-class family, Pinter first published poetry and became an actor when he left school. His first play *The Room* was performed in 1957, followed by many others, including *The Caretaker* (1960), *The Homecoming* (1964) and *No Man's Land* (1975). Pinter has also written screenplays for films, and is one of Britain's most original playwrights.

Pinter is often associated with the Theatre of the Absurd, a movement in theatre after the Second World War which explored a world which seemed to have no meaning. In Pinter's plays, the characters speak to each other in a way that seems normal and realistic. But they are always in strange situations which are never explained. This creates feelings of fear and menace that seem to come from nowhere, as horror and comedy are mixed together.

6 Parents

Text 1

1 **Think of a member of your family, and answer these questions about them:**
   - Who are they? Mother? Father? Brother? Sister? Aunt? Uncle? Grandparent? Cousin?
   - How old are they?
   - What do they look like? When you look at this person, what do you notice most about them? Their eyes, for example? Their hair? Their feet? Why?
   - When you think of this person, do you imagine any particular place? Why? Describe this place.
   - How do you feel about this person? Do you get on well with them? Do you ever dislike them? Do you feel close to them?

   Tell another student about this person in your family.

2 **Look at these two sentences:**

   Take good care of them.
   You must take good care of them.

   When can you use sentences like this?

3 Read and listen to the following poem. In the poem, who says:

'Take good care of them.'
'You must take good care of them'?

What is he or she talking about? To whom is he or she speaking?

My Father's Hands by **Jeni Couzyn**

My father's hands
are beautiful, they can
fix this moth's wing and make
machines
they can mend the fuse when the world 5
goes dark
can make light swim and walls jump
in around me again
I can see my mother's face again.

You must take good care of them with 10
your finest creams
never let the nails break or
skin go dry, only those wise fingers
know how to fix the thing
that makes my doll cry and they make 15
small animals out of clay.

Never let blades or anything sharp
and hurtful near them
don't let bees or nettles
sting them don't let fire or burning oil 20
try them

My father's hands are beautiful, take
good care of them

---

4 Add to these two lists of types of words in the poem:

verbs describing what the father's hands do fix, ...

....

nouns describing things that can hurt or harm the father's hands blades, ...

....

5 **Read and listen to the poem again, and then answer these questions:**

(a) What do we usually fix? What is fixed in line 3? What does this tell us about the father?

(b) What usually 'goes dark' (line 6)? What do you think the speaker means when she says 'the world goes dark'? How can the father 'mend the fuse'?

(c) 'can make light swim and walls jump in around me again' (lines 7–8). What do you think this sentence means? What does it tell us about the father in the poem?

(d) What does the speaker mean when she says 'I can see my mother's face again' (line 9)?

(e) As this is a poem, many capital letters (the big letters at the beginning of a sentence) and full stops (the dots at the end of a sentence) have not been used. What is the effect of leaving them out the poem?

6 **What kind of a person is the father in the poem? How does his daughter feel about him?**

Write a short paragraph about the father and his relationship with his daughter. Put it up on the walls of your classroom for other students to read.

How do *you* feel about the poem? Tell your class.

Text 2

7 **You are going to read another poem. But first look at this list of words. They are made of two other words. Can you guess what they mean?**

(a) treehouse = tree + house

(b) treetop = tree + top

(c) windbreak = wind + break

(d) windmill = wind + mill

Now match the words with these definitions:

(1) the branches at the top of a tree

(2) a tall building with parts that turn in the wind, used to grind corn, pump water etc.

(3) a wooden building in the branches of a tree for children to play in

(4) a fence or line of trees that helps to protect a place from the wind

8 **Look at these words:**

treetalk *windsong* *sugarfield*

They are not in a dictionary. They were made up by a poet. What do you think they mean? Can you write definitions for them? Read your definitions for them to your class.

9 Look at these pictures and describe what you can see in them. Then read and listen to the poem on the next page.

sugarfields by **Barbara Mahone**

treetalk and windsong
are the language of my mother
her music does not leave me.

let me taste again the cane
the syrup of the earth 5
sugarfields were once my home.

I would lie down in the fields
and never get up again
(treetalk and windsong
are the language of my mother 10
sugarfields are my home)

the leaves go on whispering secrets
as the wind blows a tune in the grass
my mother's voice is in the fields
this music cannot leave me. 15

10 What do the words treetalk, windsong and sugarfield mean in the poem? Do they have the same meaning as your definitions of these words?

11 Read and listen to the poem again, and look at the photos. Then, discuss these questions in groups:

(a) To what period in history does the poem refer?
(b) What sounds are described in the poem? How does the speaker feel about these sounds?
(c) What parts of the poem are repeated? What effect does this have?
(d) Does the mother in the poem represent anything? If so, what?
(e) Does the language and the music of the mother represent anything? If so, what?

12 Complete this sentence about the poem:

This poem makes me feel ....

because ....

Read your sentences to other students.

Creative development

Do one of the following exercises (or both if you have time).

(a) Write a short poem or description about somebody in your family, with a title like one of these:

My Father's Hands. My Mother's Eyes. My Brother's Smile.

Read it aloud to the students in your class.

(b) Look at these two groups of words:

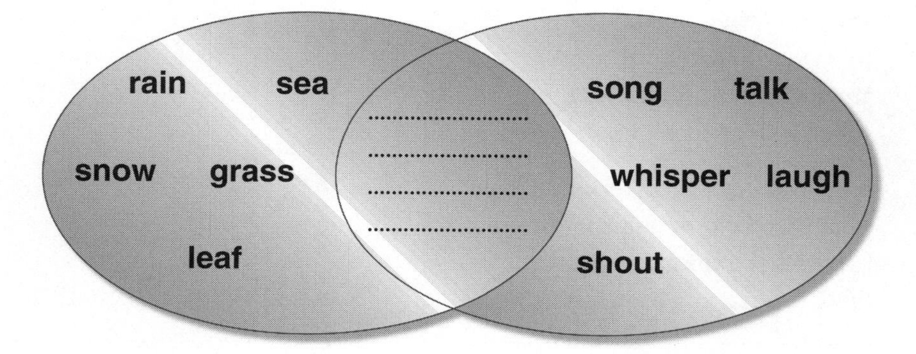

Make up some new words, by taking a word from each group, and putting them together. Think carefully about what your new words mean. Now use your words in a short poem!

Read your poem to other students. Can they guess from the poem what your new words mean?

NOTES

My Father's Hands

Vocabulary

fix (line 3): repair something that is broken

moth (line 3): an insect with wings, like a butterfly, that flies at night

fuse (line 5): a thin piece of wire in an electrical plug; it melts if there is too much power and stops any dangerous accidents

nail (line 12): the hard smooth part at the end of the fingers and toes

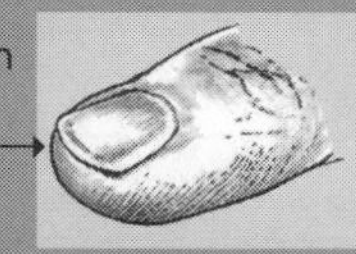

wise (line 13): having the ability to make good decisions because of your experience and understanding

clay (line 16): heavy earth that becomes hard when you bake or dry it

blade (line 17): the flat part of a knife, used for cutting

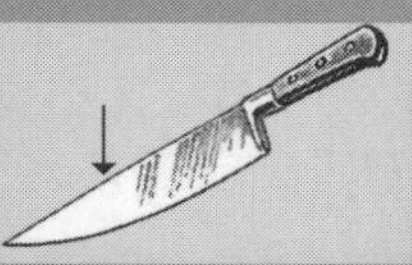

nettle (line 19): a wild plant with leaves that sting you if you touch them

Jeni Couzyn (1942–)

Poet and editor. Born and educated in South Africa, Couzyn emigrated to Britain in 1965, where she worked as a teacher and lecturer. From 1975, she spent three years in Canada before returning to Britain. Her collections of poetry include *Life by Drowning: Selected Poems* (1985). She has also edited anthologies of poetry by women.

Couzyn's poems are full of powerful images and strong rhythms. Her work explores the complex changes of identity that women experience in their lives.

sugarfields

Vocabulary

cane (line 4): the long stem of the sugar plant

syrup (line 5): a thick, sweet liquid

tune (line 13): musical notes played in a particular order

Barbara Mahone (1944–)

African American poet. Born in Chicago, Mahone's work has been published in magazines and anthologies. Her collection *sugarfields* was published in 1970.

Mahone's work celebrates the rich culture of black women, passed from mother to daughter through the oral tradition.

7 Sharing

1 How do you feel about sharing? Fill in this questionnaire.

Questionnaire

Do you find it easy to share with someone in your family, with a friend, with a stranger? What do you share with them?
Put a tick (✓) if you feel okay about sharing the things in the list. Put a cross (✗) if you don't.

	a family member	*a friend*	*a stranger*
a toothbrush			
a glass of water			
a newspaper			
a walkman			
your lunch			
a hotel room			
a taxi			
a park bench			
your life story			

Talk about the questionnaire with a partner. Give reasons for your answers.

2 *The Zoo Story* is a play about two men who meet in Central Park in New York. *Peter* is in his early forties and is wearing a suit. *Jerry* is a bit younger than Peter. He used to be handsome, but now looks tired and badly dressed.

You are going to read an extract from the play. Here are three possible titles for the extract:

A visit to the zoo
The fight
A new friend

As you read and listen to the text, think about which title is best.

---

from *The Zoo Story* by **Edward Albee**

JERRY Now I'll let you in on what happened at the zoo; but first, I should tell you why I went to the zoo. I went to the zoo to find out more about the way people exist with animals, and the way animals exist with each other, and with people too. It probably wasn't a fair test, what with everyone separated by bars from everyone else, the animals for the most part from each other, and always the people from the animals. But, if it's a zoo, that's the way it is. (*He pokes* PETER *on the arm.*) Move over. 5

PETER (*friendly*) I'm sorry, haven't you enough room? (*He shifts a little.*)

JERRY (*smiling slightly*) Well, all the animals are there, and all the people are there, and it's Sunday and all the children are there. (*He pokes* PETER *again.*) Move over. 10

PETER (*patiently, still friendly*) All right.

(*He moves some more, and* JERRY *has all the room he might need.*)

JERRY And it's a hot day, so all the stench is there, too, and all the balloon sellers, and all the ice-cream sellers, and all the seals are barking, and all the birds are screaming. (*Pokes* PETER *harder.*) Move over! 15

PETER (*beginning to be annoyed*) Look here, you have more than enough room! (*But he moves more, and is now fairly cramped at one end of the bench.*)

JERRY And I am there, and it's feeding time at the lion's house, and the lion keeper comes into the lion cage, one of the lion cages, to feed one of the lions. (*Punches* PETER *on the arm, hard.*) MOVE OVER! 20

PETER (*very annoyed*) I can't move over any more, and stop hitting me. What's the matter with you?

JERRY Do you want to hear the story? (*Punches* PETER*'s arm again.*)

PETER (*flabbergasted*) I'm not so sure! I certainly don't want to be punched in the arm. 25

JERRY (*Punches* PETER*'s arm again.*) Like that?

PETER Stop it. What's the matter with you?

JERRY I'm crazy, you bastard.

PETER That isn't funny.

JERRY	Listen to me, Peter. I want this bench. You go sit on the bench over there, and if you're good I'll tell you the rest of the story.	30
PETER	(*flustered*) But ... what ever for? What *is* the matter with you? Besides, I see no reason why I should give up this bench. I sit on this bench almost every Sunday afternoon, in good weather. It's secluded here; there's never anyone sitting here, so I have it all to myself.	35
JERRY	(*softly*) Get off this bench, Peter; I want it.	
PETER	(*almost whining*) No.	
JERRY	I said I want this bench, and I'm going to have it. Now get over there.	
PETER	People can't have everything they want. You should know that; it's a rule; people can have some of the things they want, but they can't have everything.	40
JERRY	(*laughs*) Imbecile! You're slow-witted!	
PETER	Stop that!	
JERRY	You're a vegetable! Go lie on the ground.	
PETER	(*intense*) Now *you* listen to me.	

---

3 Which title do you think is best for this extract? Why?
Discuss your ideas with a partner.
Can you suggest any other title for the extract?

4 Look at these three words that describe things you can *do*:

push *hit* *move*

Can you use them to complete the following definitions:

(a) *to poke* (line 6): to .... someone with something sharp, like your fingers or your elbow
(b) *to shift* (line 8): to .... your place or position
(c) *to punch* (line 21): to .... someone or something hard with your closed hand

Look at these words that describe *feelings*:

nervous *surprised* *angry*

Can you use them to complete the following definitions:

(d) *annoyed* (line 17): quite .... or cross
(e) *flabbergasted* (line 25): very ....
(f) *flustered* (line 32): confused and ....

5 In the text, Jerry tries to get and keep power over Peter. He does this in different ways. Look at these tables with some ideas about how Jerry does this:

Jerry tries to control Peter *physically*
What he does
1 He pokes Peter (lines 6, 10, 16)
2

Jerry tries to control Peter *with his words*	
	What he says
He shares a secret with Peter	I'll let you in on what happened at the zoo (line 1)
He orders Peter to do things	
He shouts at Peter	
He makes Peter give him attention	
He behaves as if Peter is a child	
He repeats what he wants a few times	
He describes Peter in a rude way	

Read and listen to the text again, and try to fill in the tables with examples. Are there any other ways that Jerry tries to get what he wants?

6 How does Peter react to Jerry? What does he do or say to answer Jerry? Complete this paragraph:

In the beginning, Peter ....

....

But then ....

....

....

7 **Look at this list of adjectives. Use a dictionary to help you choose some that describe Peter and some that describe Jerry:**

lonely aggressive selfish respectable caring passive

unselfish crazy angry kind reasonable friendly

8 **Answer these questions:**

(a) In this extract Jerry does not finish his story about going to the zoo. What do you think happened to him at the zoo?

(b) How do Jerry and Peter feel about sharing the park bench? Would you behave in the same way as Peter? What would you do if you met somebody like Jerry in a park?

(c) Why do you think the play is called *The Zoo Story*?

(d) Do you think a conversation like the one between Jerry and Peter could really happen? Why?

Creative development

In pairs or groups, talk about what you think happens next in the play. Prepare a short *mime* of what you think happens. Do your mime for your class.

Then choose the mime you like the best, and write a short dialogue (about 6–10 lines) between Peter and Jerry (and other people?) based on the mime. Read your dialogues to your class.

Then, if you want to know what happens in the actual play, look in the key at the back of the book.

NOTES

Vocabulary

I'll let you in on (line 1): I'll tell you something nobody else knows

exist (line 3): live

a fair test (line 4): a test that treats everybody in an equal way

separated (line 4): kept apart from each other

stench (line 14): a strong and unpleasant smell

cramped (line 18): not having a lot of room

bastard (line 28): a person who has behaved very badly; it is used in informal, spoken English and many people think it is very rude

I have it all to myself (line 35): I'm the only person using it

whining (line 37): complaining, in a sad and annoying way

imbecile (line 41): very stupid person

slow-witted (line 41): very stupid

intense (line 44): having very strong feelings

Edward Albee (1928–)

American playwright. Albee did many different jobs before his first play *The Zoo Story* was produced in Germany in 1959. It later became a great success in New York City. He has written many plays that have been performed all over the world, including *The Death of Bessie Smith* (1962) and *Who's Afraid of Virginia Woolf?* (1964).

Albee's plays deal with how difficult it is for people to find meaning in their lives and to communicate with each other. Like Pinter he is often associated with the Theatre of the Absurd (see Unit 5). In his plays, he mixes humour with stronger feelings, such as fear. He creates dialogue that seems to be strange and mysterious, but at the same time as natural as real conversation.

8 Memories

1 Here is someone's sketch of some of the important *facts* of their life. Can you guess what these are from the sketch?

2 Read this short paragraph about the sketch above.

Autobiography

I was born in Bristol on 15 February 1955, the youngest of three children. When I was five, my family moved to London where I grew up and went to school. I left school at sixteen, and started working at a bakery. Now I live in Greece where I own a small restaurant. I am married with one daughter.

Were your guesses about the sketch correct?

3 Now make a quick sketch of some of the important *facts* of your life.

4 In pairs, look at each other's 'Life' sketches. Ask each other questions about them. Use these ideas to help you:

Where/you/born?
When/you/born?
Where/you/grow/up?
Where/live/now? etc

If you do not want to answer any of the questions, say to your partner 'I'm sorry, I prefer not to answer that question.'

5 Can you write a short paragraph about the *facts* of your life or of someone you know. Give it to your teacher and other students to read. Answer any questions they have about it.

6 Read and listen to this poem called *Autobiography*. While you read and listen write down any *facts* about the speaker's life.

Autobiography by **Louis MacNeice**

In my childhood trees were green
And there was plenty to be seen.

Come back early or never come.

My father made the walls resound,
He wore his collar the wrong way round. 5

Come back early or never come.

My mother wore a yellow dress;
Gently, gently, gentleness.

Come back early or never come.

When I was five the black dreams came; 10
Nothing after was quite the same.

Come back early or never come.

The dark was talking to the dead;
The lamp was dark beside my bed.

Come back early or never come. 15

When I woke they did not care;
Nobody, nobody was there.

Come back early or never come.

When my silent terror cried,
Nobody, nobody replied. 20

Come back early or never come.

I got up; the chilly sun
Saw me walk away alone.

Come back early or never come.

---

7 In the poem, we find words connected with *light* and words connected with *dark*. What do the words *light* and *dark* make you think of? How do these words make you feel?
Write down your ideas below.

Talk to another student about your ideas.
Now read and listen to the poem again. What words in the poem are connected with *light*? What words in the poem are connected with *dark*? Were any of the words in the poem the same as your ideas or feelings above? Which ones?

8 Here is the poem with some handwritten questions written on it. In pairs, talk about the questions. Give your own ideas to answer them.

Autobiography

In my childhood trees were green What does this colour make you think of?
And there was plenty to be seen. What kind of childhood did the speaker have?

Come back early or never come. Did somebody go away? And never come back? Who?

filled the room with noise? How?
My father made the walls resound, How did the child feel about this?
He wore his collar the wrong way round. Why? His job? 5

Come back early or never come. Repeated. Why?

My mother wore a yellow dress; What does this colour make you think of?
Gently, gently, gentleness. How did child feel about the mother?

Come back early or never come. Repeated. Why?

When I was five the black dreams came; What were they about? 10
Nothing after was quite the same. How did the child feel?

Come back early or never come.

What does this mean?
The dark was talking to the dead;
The lamp was dark beside my bed. Repeated word – dark. Effect?

Come back early or never come. 15

When I woke they did not care; Who?
Nobody, nobody was there. Repeated. Why?

Come back early or never come.

What does this mean?
When my silent terror cried,
Nobody, nobody replied. 20
Repeated. Why?

Come back early or never come.

What does this mean?
I got up; the chilly sun
Saw me walk away alone. How did the child feel?

Come back early or never come. Final repetition. Effect?

9 Talk about these questions:

(a) 'The dark was talking to the dead' (line 13). The dark is described as if it was a person; this is called *personification*. What is the effect of describing 'the dark' in this way? Can you find any other examples of personification in the poem?

(b) 'the chilly sun' (line 22). How can a sun be chilly? This is a *paradox* (words that do not seem to make sense because they contain two ideas that are opposite to each other). What is the effect of describing the sun in this way? Can you find any other examples of paradox in the poem?

10 Read these facts about Louis MacNeice's life:

Louis MacNeice's unfinished autobiography *The Strings are False* was published in 1965. In it we learn that MacNeice's mother was a calm, comforting person to whom he was very close and with whom he spent a lot of time. In March 1913, when he was five, she had an operation. She was still loving and gentle to her children, but she changed into a very unhappy and nervous woman. In August 1913, she went away to a nursing-home in Dublin. MacNeice never saw her again. She died of tuberculosis in December 1914.

Does this information change how you understand the poem *Autobiography*?
In what way?
Do you like the poem? Why?

Creative development

A critic once said that 'colour, shape, light and shade, sound, smell, touch and taste' make the *time* and *place* in Louis MacNeice's poems seem very real.

Give yourself five quiet minutes to remember something from when you were five or six years old. Don't think about *facts* too much. Instead think about:

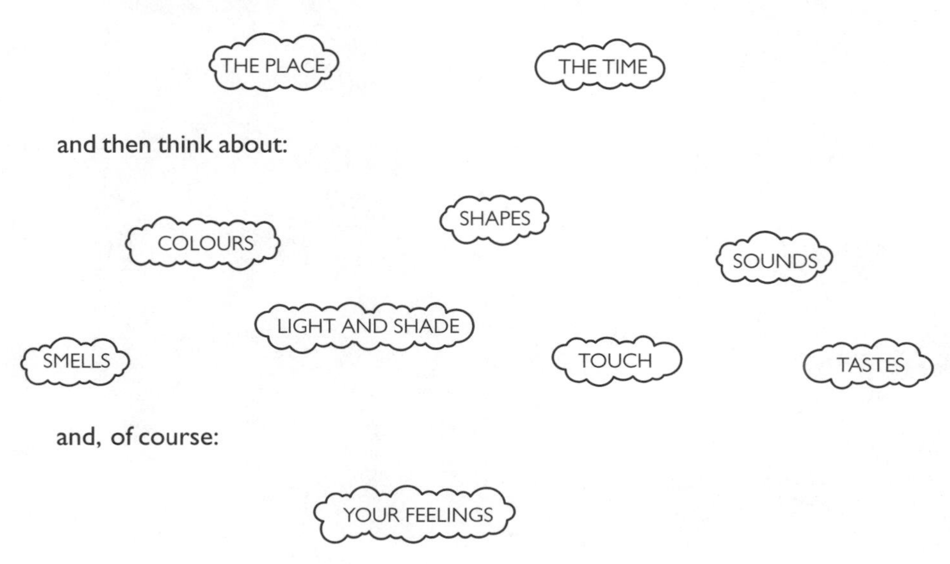

and, of course:

YOUR FEELINGS

Write down some words and sentences about this memory. Then, either tell another student about this memory, or write a short paragraph about it.

NOTES

Vocabulary

autobiography: a text somebody writes about their own life

childhood (line 1): the time in your life when you are a child

collar (line 5): the part of a shirt, dress or coat that fits round your neck

gentle (line 8): kind and calm

gentleness (line 8): the quality of being kind and calm

silent (line 19): without any noise

terror (line 19): a feeling of being very afraid

chilly (line 22): quite cold

Louis MacNeice (1907–1963)

British poet and writer of radio plays. Born in Northern Ireland, the son of a Protestant bishop, Louis MacNeice was educated at Oxford University where he was associated with the left-wing poets Stephen Spender and W. H. Auden. During and after the Second World War, he wrote radio plays for the BBC. He also wrote two travel books (one with W. H. Auden), stories for children and many books of poetry, including *Collected Poems* (1966).

In his poems, MacNeice experimented with many classical forms, but especially different kinds of rhyme, and the repetitions common in the Irish songs and poems of his childhood. His poems are full of strong sensory images, put together with delicate care.

9 *Maids and madams*

Text 1

1 You are going to read part of a story called *The Lady's Maid* which describes a time when rich people in England had many servants. The story is told by a woman, Ellen, who has worked as a maid since she was 13 years old. What kind of work did a lady's maid do? Use the pictures above to help you. Write down your ideas:

....

....

....

2 Write two sentences about the life of a lady's maid. Use these ideas to help you.

A lady's maid was
- part of the family.
- a person doing an honest job.
- a kind of slave.
- often her lady's closest friend.

Talk to the other students about your ideas. Do you agree with each other?

3 In the story, the lady's maid Ellen is talking to someone she calls 'madam'. Ellen tells 'the madam' how she, Ellen, had planned to marry a young man called Harry many years before. He owned a flower-shop, near where Ellen was living with 'her lady' (the woman she worked for as a maid).

Did Ellen marry Harry?

Read and listen to the story to find out.

---

from *The Lady's Maid* by **Katherine Mansfield**

The day came he was to call for me to choose the furniture. Shall I ever forget it? It was a Tuesday. My lady wasn't quite herself that afternoon. Not that she'd said anything, of course; she never does or will. But I knew by the way that she kept wrapping herself up and asking me if it was cold – and her little nose looked ... pinched. I didn't like leaving her; I knew I'd be worrying all the time. At last I asked her if she'd rather I put it off. 'Oh no, Ellen' she said, 'you musn't mind about me. You musn't disappoint your young man.' And so cheerful, you know, madam, never thinking about herself. It made me feel worse than ever. I began to wonder ... then she dropped her handkerchief and began to stoop down to pick it up herself – a thing she never did. 'Whatever are you doing!' I cried, running to stop her. 'Well,' she said, smiling, you know, madam, 'I shall have to begin to practise.' Oh, it was all I could do not to burst out crying. I went over to the dressing-table and made believe to rub up the silver, and I couldn't keep myself in, and I asked her if she'd rather I ... didn't get married. 'No, Ellen' she said – that was her voice, madam, like I'm giving you – 'No, Ellen, not for the *wide world*!' But while she said it, madam – I was looking in her glass; of course, she didn't know I could see her – she put her little hand on her heart just like her dear mother used to, and lifted her eyes ... Oh, *madam*

When Harry came I had his letters all ready, and the ring and the ducky little brooch he'd given me – a silver bird it was, with a chain in its beak, and on the end of the chain a heart with a dagger. Quite the thing! I opened the door to him. I never gave him time for a word. 'There you are,' I said. 'Take them all back,' I said, 'it's all over. I'm not going to marry you,' I said, 'I can't leave my lady.' White! He turned as white as a woman. I had to slam the door, and there I stood, all of a tremble, till I knew he had gone. When I opened the door – believe me or not, madam – that man *was* gone! I ran out into the road just as I was, in my apron and my houseshoes, and there I stayed in the middle of the road ... staring.

---

4 Can you match these words or expressions in the text with the correct definition:

(1) to call for someone (line 1)
(2) to be yourself (line 2)
(3) to put something off (line 7)
(4) to mind about someone (line 8)
(5) It was all I could do not to burst out crying (line 14)
(6) I couldn't keep myself in (line 16)
(7) not for the wide world (line 18)
(8) it's all over (lines 26–7)

(a) to feel alright, in both your body and your mind
(b) I almost couldn't stop myself from crying
(c) I couldn't stop myself from saying something
(d) to worry about someone
(e) to come and fetch someone so that you can go anywhere together
(f) to arrange to do something later
(g) not for anything
(h) it's finished

5 True or False?

(a) Before she got married, Ellen went to choose some furniture with Harry.
(b) On that day, her lady was ill in bed.
(c) Her lady said that she wanted Ellen to go out with Harry.
(d) Ellen's lady always picked up the things that she dropped.
(e) Ellen pretended to clean the silver so that she did not start crying.
(f) Her lady said that Ellen should marry Harry.
(g) When Harry came, Ellen spoke to him for a long time.
(h) Ellen only gave Harry back his letters.
(i) Ellen told Harry that she did not love him any more.
(j) Ellen ran into the road and called to Harry.

6 In the story, Ellen describes what her lady said or did. But perhaps the lady really *meant* something different. Read and listen to the text again. Then, in groups, write down your ideas about the lady's behaviour.

What the lady said/did	*What the lady really wanted*
The lady asked Ellen if it was cold; she wrapped herself up.	She wanted Ellen to think that she wasn't well, and feel sorry for her? Then, Ellen might stay with her.
She said that Ellen must go out with Harry and not disappoint him.	
She dropped her handkerchief, and picked it up herself. She said that she needed to practise because Ellen was going away.	
She said that she wanted Ellen to get married. She put her hand on her heart, and lifted her eyes.	

7 Discuss these questions in groups:

- Ellen says this about her lady: 'And so cheerful, you know, madam, never thinking about herself' (lines 8–9). Do you agree with Ellen's idea about her lady?
- Was Ellen right or wrong not to marry Harry?
- Who is the 'madam' that Ellen is talking to in the story? Why do you think that Ellen is telling her the story?

8 The story of *The Lady's Maid* is told from the maid's *point of view* (i.e. how Ellen, the maid, sees and understands what happened). But other characters in the story might understand things in a different way.

Imagine you are Harry. How did *he* feel about what happened? What did he think about Ellen's 'lady'? Imagine he is talking to the 'madam' in the story. Write a paragraph in which he describes his feelings to her. Begin like this:

So, then Madam, we planned to go out on the Tuesday ....

....

....

....

....

....

OR

Imagine you are the 'lady' in the story. How did she feel about Ellen's plans to marry Harry? How did she feel when Ellen decided not to marry Harry? Imagine she is talking to the 'madam' in the story. Write a short paragraph in which she describes her feelings. Begin like this:

So, then you see, my dear, Ellen told me her news. She wanted to marry Harry

and ....

....

....

....

....

Text 2

9 You are going to read a poem about a maid, which comes from a collection called *Madam to You* by Langston Hughes, an American writer. The speaker in all the poems in the collection is a poor black woman with a very strong character, called Alberta K. Johnson. She does many different jobs in her life, including working as a maid. She always wants people to show respect towards her, and so she calls herself madam, and expects other people to call her madam too.

Read and listen to her describing her life as a maid:

Madam and her Madam by **Langston Hughes**

I worked for a woman,
She wasn't mean –
But she had a twelve-room
House to clean.

Had to get breakfast, 5
Dinner, and supper, too –
Then take care of her children
When I got through.

Wash, iron, and scrub,
Walk the dog around – 10
It was too much,
Nearly broke me down.

I said, Madam,
Can it be
You're trying to make a 15
Pack-horse out of me?

She opened her mouth.
She cried, Oh no!
You know, Alberta,
I love you so! 20

I said, Madam,
That may be true –
But I'll be dogged
If I love you!

---

10 Answer these questions:

(a) How did Alberta feel about her work?
(b) How did the 'madam' feel about Alberta?
(c) How did Alberta feel about her 'madam'?
(d) *Madam and her Madam*. Can you explain the title of the poem?
(e) Which words in the poem rhyme? What effect does the rhyme have?

11 In groups write some notes about Ellen, the lady's maid, and Alberta K. Johnson.

How Ellen and Alberta are the same	*How they are different*

Who do you *like* more? Ellen or Alberta?
Who do you *respect* more? Ellen or Alberta?
Which *text* do you prefer? Why?

Creative development

Imagine that Alberta's 'Madam' is moving to another town. Another family is thinking about giving Alberta a job as a maid. They want to know about Alberta's character and abilities. Imagine you are Alberta's 'Madam'. What do you think about her? Complete this letter about Alberta.

Mrs Harriet Delancey, 135 River Drive, Alabama

To whom it may concern

Alberta Jones worked for me for .... Her work involved ....
....
She also .... and .... I think she is a .... person, who .... She ....
....
....

Yours sincerely

Mrs Harriet Delancey

Read the letters of the other students in your class. Would you give Alberta a job? Why?

NOTES

The Lady's Maid

Vocabulary

wrapping herself up (line 4): putting warm clothes on herself

pinched (line 5): thin and unhealthy

cheerful (line 9): behaving in a way that shows you are happy

stoop down (line 11): bend the body forward and down

made believe (line 15): pretended

rub up (line 15): move and press a cloth over something to make it clean and shining

the silver (line 15): objects made from silver, like knives, forks, spoons and dishes (in this case, probably little dishes or other silver ornaments)

glass (line 19): an old-fashioned word for a mirror

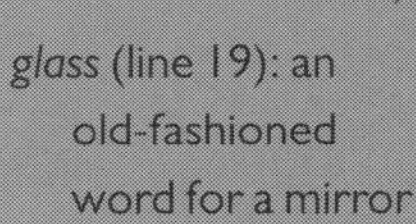

ducky (line 23): an old-fashioned way of saying lovely

brooch (line 23): a piece of jewellery that women fasten to their clothes with a pin

dagger (line 24): a short, pointed knife used in the past as a weapon

slam (line 28): close very loudly

to tremble (line 29): to shake because you are cold, afraid or upset

Katherine Mansfield (1888–1923)

Short story writer. Born in New Zealand, she went to England in 1903. In 1911, her first collection of short stories was published, and she published another four books of stories during her life. She spent the last eight years of her life travelling in Europe, to try to cure the tuberculosis from which she died.

Mansfield's short stories were very original, and she changed the short story in English. The stories show a deep interest in everyday life, and a delicate sense of form. Many of them are based on her childhood experiences and family in New Zealand, but she also wrote about the European society of the time.

Madam and her Madam

Vocabulary

mean (line 2): unkind, not generous

got through (line 8): finished

scrub (line 9): clean something by rubbing it hard

broke me down (line 12): made me ill, both in body and mind

pack-horse (line 16): a horse that is used to carry heavy things

I'll be dogged if … (line 23): an old-fashioned American English phrase used when you are very sure that you won't do something

Langston Hughes (1902–1967)

African American writer. As a young man, Hughes had many jobs, including working as a teacher, a seaman, and a night-club cook. He published many collections of poetry and short stories, plays, screenplays, two autobiographies and many books on historical and musical subjects. He also worked as a journalist, and started three black theatre companies.

Hughes tried to use the oral traditions of black culture in written form, for example by using jazz rhythms in his poems. During the 1930s his writing became more political, as he supported the struggle of African Americans against racism. His writings are full of humour and show a sharp eye for detail.

10 Music and birdsong

1 Imagine you are going for a walk in the countryside, away from the city. Talk to another student about it:

(a) Would you prefer to go alone or with other people? Why?
(b) Where would you go? Near to where you live? In another part of your country? Why?

Now, imagine the *countryside* around you – hills? mountains? a river? a forest? sky? clouds? etc.

Imagine the *colours* of the countryside.
Imagine the *plants, flowers and trees* you might see.
Imagine the *animals* or *birds* you might see.
Imagine the *sounds* you might hear.

Close your eyes for two to three minutes. In your mind, take a walk through this countryside.
At the end of your walk, how do you feel?

2 You are going to read and listen to a short story by Janet Frame, a writer from New Zealand. In the story, a walk through the New Zealand countryside is described.
Look at this picture of New Zealand. Is the countryside in this photo at all the same as the countryside you imagined? In what way?

Read and listen to the story.

The Birds Began to Sing by **Janet Frame**

The birds began to sing. There were four and twenty of them singing, and they were blackbirds.

And I said, what are you singing all day and night, in the sun and the dark and the rain, and in the wind that turns the tops of the trees silver? 5

We are singing, they said. We are singing and we have just begun, and we've a long way to sing, and we can't stop, we've got to go on and on. Singing.

The birds began to sing.

I put on my coat and I walked in the rain over the hills. I walked 10 through swamps full of red water, and down gullies covered in snowberries, and then up gullies again, with snow grass growing there, and speargrass, and over creeks near flax and tussock and manuka.

I saw a pine tree on top of a hill. 15

I saw a skylark dipping and rising.

I saw it was snowing somewhere over the hills, but not where I was.

I stood on a hill and looked and looked.

I wasn't singing. I tried to sing but I couldn't think of the song. 20

So I went back home to the boarding house where I live, and I sat on the stairs in the front and I listened. I listened with my head and my eyes and my brain and my hands. With my body.

The birds began to sing.

They were blackbirds sitting on the telegraph wires and hopping 25 on the apple trees. There were four and twenty of them singing.

What is the song? I said. Tell me the name of the song.

I am a human being and I read books and I hear music and I like to see things in print. I like to see *vivace andante* words by music by performed by written for. So I said what is the name of the song, tell 30 me and I will write it and you can listen at my window when I get the finest musicians in the country to play it, and you will feel so nice to hear your song so tell me the name.

They stopped singing. It was dark outside although the sun was shining. It was dark and there was no more singing. 35

3 Here are some of the feelings that people had after they read the story:

lovely descriptions

difficult to understand

not real

strange, but beautiful

full of poetry

What did you feel about the story after you read it? Talk to other students about your feelings.

4 Look at these lines from the text:

I put on my coat and walked in the rain over the hills. I walked through *swamps* full of red water, and down *gullies* covered in snowberries, and then up *gullies* again, with snow grass growing there, and speargrass, and over *creeks* near flax and tussock and manuka. 10

I saw a pine tree on top of a hill. 15
I saw a skylark dipping and rising.

Which of the words in italics mean:

(a) an area of land that is soft and wet?
(b) a small, narrow stream of water?
(c) a small, narrow valley between two hills?

What other words in the text helped you to decide their meaning?

(d) Write down all the names of trees or plants in lines 10–15.
(e) If a skylark is a type of bird, what do you think the words *dipping* and *rising* (line 16) mean?

5 Answer these questions:

- What did the speaker twice ask the blackbirds?
- What was the answer the first time?
- What was the answer the second time?

6 Read and listen to the text again, and then discuss these questions:

(a) 'I listened with my head and my eyes and my brain and my hands. With my body' (lines 22–3). What does this mean?

(b) 'I like to see *vivace andante* words by music by performed by written for' (lines 29–30). Is there anything unusual about the grammar in this sentence? What is the effect of using the word 'by' so many times?

(c) The sentence in lines 30 to 33 is very long. Is this sentence unusual in any way? How it different from the sentence that follows (line 34)? What effect does this have?

(d) Look at the last paragraph of the story (lines 34–5). Why do you think the birds did not sing anymore? How could it be dark if the sun was still shining?

7 Think about the story, and then give your ideas:
How is the song of the blackbirds different to the music of the finest musicians?

8 Here are some ideas about what the story means (i.e. the *theme* of the story). Do you agree with them? Why? Write your own ideas about what the story means.

- Nature is very beautiful, but people often forget this.
- Art can never be as beautiful as nature.
- People spoil nature by wanting to own it.
- ....
- ....

Talk to the other students in your class about your ideas.

Creative development

Use your own ideas to complete this questionnaire.

Do you prefer

(a) the song of blackbirds OR the music of the finest musicians?
(b) a pine tree OR a poem?
(c) .... OR ....?
(d) .... OR ....?
(e) .... OR ....?

Ask other students in your class the five questions in your questionnaire. Answer their questions. Explain what you prefer, and why.

NOTES

Vocabulary

four and twenty (line 1): we usually say twenty-four; four and twenty blackbirds comes from a children's rhyme in English called 'Sing a song of sixpence'

blackbird (line 2): a common European and North American bird; the male is completely black

skylark (line 16): a small bird that sings while flying very high

boarding house (line 21): a private house where you pay to have a room

telegraph wires (line 25): wires that were used to send messages in an old-fashioned way by radio or electrical signals

in print (line 29): printed in a book or newspaper, etc.

vivace (line 29): a word used in music to show that you should play something in a quick, lively way

andante (line 29): quite slowly (a word used in music)

finest (line 32): best

Janet Frame (1924–)

New Zealand novelist. One of five children from a very poor family, she had a difficult childhood. Two of her sisters drowned when young. She started training to be a teacher, but from 1947 she spent seven years in mental hospitals. During this time, she published a collection of stories called *The Lagoon*. Frame has written eleven novels, three volumes of autobiography, four collections of short stories, a collection of poetry and a children's book.

Frame's early writing (e.g. *The Lagoon*) deals with how childhood and the imagination can be destroyed by death and society. In her later work, she explores the power of language and its relation to what is true. Many of her characters do not fit easily into society (e.g. they are artists or they are mad), and they try to use language to find out who they really are.

11 Growing older

Text 1

1 **Read these sentences:**

- Old people can teach young people a lot about life.
- Old people only want to talk about what happened many years ago.
- Old people don't have enough power to decide what they want to do.
- Old people should always live with their families.

Do you agree with these sentences? Why?

Write two sentences yourself. Talk to other students about your sentences. Do you agree or disagree with each other?

2 Look at this chart about three people in a play.

old woman called

....

her daughter-in-law called

....

her son called

....

Read and listen to the extract from the play, and fill in the names of the people.

---

from *The Porch* by **Jennifer Johnston**

HELEN You pour out Frank. I'll sit on this little stool next to mother. That'll be cosy, won't it? All of us having a nice cup of tea together. She said she had a visitor today.

FRANK Really? Who was that Mother? Who?

HELEN She isn't listening. Her eyes go all funny when she isn't listening. Give her a piece of cake. 5

FRANK Cake, Mother?

MAUD It was the man upstairs.

HELEN There isn't a man upstairs. No one upstairs. There isn't an upstairs, unless you count the box room. Haha. No man there. Have this nice bit of cake. 10

FRANK God. She means God. She always used to call Him the man Upstairs. I used to get so worried when I was small. Puzzled. Like you, I thought someone must be hiding in the box room. She used to say 'I'll just have a few words about it with the man upstairs.' Didn't you mother?

MAUD Did you make it mother? 15

HELEN Helen ... Yes, I made it especially for you.

MAUD That's very kind of you. Very kind indeed to go to so much trouble. Double trouble double ...

HELEN No bother.

MAUD Such strange things dance in my mind. Strange words come ... What will happen to the cat? 20

FRANK We'll take the cat. Don't worry your head about the cat. We'll give her a good home.

MAUD She might knock things off the mantlepiece.

FRANK Don't you worry about her. 25

MAUD She'll probably die.

FRANK I shouldn't think so. Cats are very adaptable beasts.

She'll settle in a week or so.

MAUD She and I?

FRANK You'll settle. You know you'll settle. 30

MAUD There's no use buying her Kit-e-kat. She doesn't eat it. She'd starve herself to death rather than eat it. She's funny like that. She'll sniff at it and then walk away. Angry. It makes her really angry if you give her Kit-e-kat. Tell her.

FRANK Who?

MAUD Your wife. Tell your wife not to waste her money on that stuff. 35

FRANK She's here mother. This is Helen.

MAUD I don't know. I called her mother.

HELEN But I told you I was Helen.

MAUD You called me mother.

HELEN Yes I've always called you mother. 40

MAUD It all comes to the same thing in the end.

taken from *The Nightingale Not the Lark* (1988)

---

3 **Complete these sentences about some of the words in the text:**

	Meaning
line 13–14 'I'll just have a few words about it to the man upstairs.'	(a) I'll just .... about it to the man upstairs.
line 17 'Very kind indeed to go to much trouble.'	(b) It's very kind of you to .... so much time to do this.
line 22 'Don't worry your head about the cat.'	(c) Don't be so unhappy that you .... about it all the time.

4 **Which summary of the text is the best?**

(a) A husband and wife visit the husband's old mother. They have a cup of tea together. They are taking the old woman's cat home with them, because the old woman doesn't want to look after it any more.
(b) A husband and wife visit the husband's old mother. They have a cup of tea together. Then they will take the cat to a home for animals, because the old woman doesn't want to look after it any longer.
(c) A husband and wife visit the husband's old mother. They have a cup of tea together. They plan to take the mother to a home for old people, and the cat home with them.

5 **Read and listen to the text again. Then complete this exercise.**

Here are some words from the play. Some of them have a ring around them. Who is meant by the words in the ring? Maud, Frank, Helen or the cat?

A

HELEN All of us having a nice cup of tea together. She said she had a visitor today.
FRANK Really? Who was that Mother? Who?
HELEN She isn't listening. Her eyes go all funny when she isn't listening. 5

B

MAUD Did you make it mother? 15

C

MAUD It makes her really angry if you give her Kit-e-kat. Tell her

FRANK Who?

MAUD Your wife. Tell your wife not to waste money on that stuff. 35

In groups, discuss these questions:

A Maud is sitting next to Frank and Helen in the same room. So, why do they call her 'she' rather than 'you'?

B Why does Maud call Helen 'mother'?

C Why does Maud talk to Frank *about* Helen, calling her 'your wife', instead of talking to Helen herself?

6 What do we learn about Maud (her character and feelings) from these parts of the text?

(a) She had a visit from 'the man upstairs'. (line 8)

(b) She says 'Such strange things dance in my mind.' (line 20)

(c) She talks a lot about her cat. (lines 31–3)

(d) She says that 'It all comes to the same thing in the end.' (line 41)

7 How do Maud, Helen and Frank feel in the play? Complete their thoughts:

I'm leaving my home now, and I feel ....

Frank's mother is leaving her home now, and I feel ....

Mother's leaving now, and I feel ....

Compare your ideas with the other students in your class. Who do you feel the most sorry for – Maud, Helen or Frank?

Text 2

8 You are going to read a poem called *A Proud Old Man (Grandpa)*. What do you think a proud old man does? Finish these sentences:

A proud old man always ....

A proud old man never ....

Share your ideas with other students.

9 *A Proud Old Man (Grandpa)* is written by Paul Chidyausiku, a poet from Zimbabwe. In the poem, an old African man describes his life both now and many years ago.

Read and listen to the poem:

A Proud Old Man (Grandpa) by **Paul Chidyausiku**

They say they are healthier
than me,
Though they can't walk to the
end of a mile.
At their age I walked forty at night (5)
to wage battle at dawn.
They think they are healthier
than me.
If their socks get wet they
catch cold, (10)
When my sockless feet got wet,
I never sneezed,
But they still think that they are
healthier than me.
On a soft mattress (15)
over a spring bed
They still have to take a sleeping
pill.
But I, with reeds cutting into my
ribs (20)
My head resting on a piece of
wood,
I sleep like a baby and snore.

Are your sentences about a proud old man the same as the proud old man in the poem?

10 Who are 'they' in the poem?

11 Read and listen to the poem again. Then, fill in this table:

What the grandpa did/does	*What 'they' do*

How does the grandpa feel about 'they'? And how do 'they' feel about him? Talk to other students about your ideas.

12 Which text do you prefer? The one about Maud? Or the one about the Proud Old Man? Why?

Creative development

Can you write a poem about an old person?
Call your poem *The Angry Old Man/Woman* or *The Happy Old Man/Woman* or *The Kind Old Man/Woman*. Or perhaps you can give your poem another title? Then, use this outline to help you write your poem:

They say they ....

....

Though ....

....

At their age ....

....

They think they ....

....

If their ....

....

But I ....

....

Read your poems aloud to the other students in the class, but do *not* give the title of your poem. Can the other students guess what the title is?

NOTES

The Porch

Vocabulary

pour out (line 1): pour tea into cups

stool (line 1): a seat with legs but no back

cosy (line 1): warm and comfortable

box room (line 10): a small room where you keep things you are not using

puzzled (line 12): confused and not able to understand something

knock (line 24): hit something so that it moves or falls

mantlepiece (line 24): the shelf above a fireplace

adaptable (line 27): able to change your behaviour in different situations

beast (line 27): an old-fashioned word for an animal

settle (line 30): get used to a new place

Kit-e-kat (line 33): the name of a kind of cat food

starve herself to death (lines 31–2): die from refusing to eat

sniff (line 32): breathe in to smell something

Jennifer Johnston (1930–)

Irish novelist and playwright. Born in Dublin, the daughter of an actress and a playwright, Jennifer Johnston lives in Northern Ireland. She has written many novels, a play and some short dramatic pieces collected in *The Nightingale Not the Lark*.

Johnson's novels deal with how politics and violence can destroy private relationships, for example those between Catholics and Protestants. They also explore how love and loyalty can give us hope. She writes in a simple, exact way which catches the rhythm of how people speak.

A Proud Old Man (Grandpa)

Vocabulary

healthy (line 1): strong and well

wage battle (line 6): fight your enemy (an old-fashioned way of saying this)

catch cold (line 10): get an illness which causes coughs and sneezes and sometimes headache and a fever

mattress (line 15): the part of a bed that makes it comfortable to lie on – it is made of a strong cloth cover filled with firm material

spring bed (line 16): a bed with springs. A spring is a long, thin piece of metal that bends round, but goes back to its usual shape after you press it down

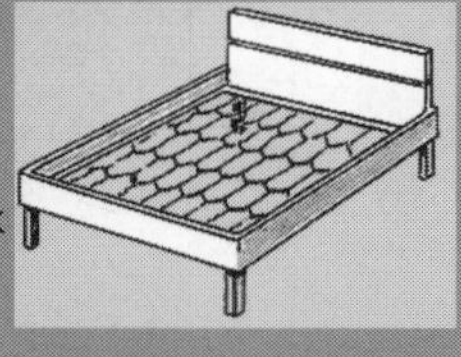

reed (line 19): tall plants like grass that grow in groups near water

rib (line 20): one of twelve bones that curve round from the back to the chest

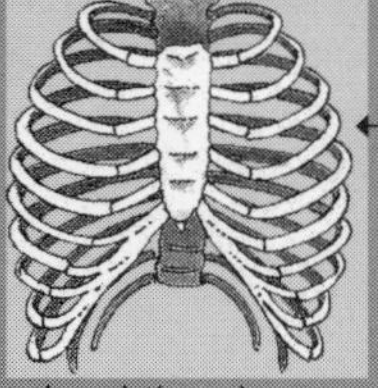

snore (line 23): breathe noisily while asleep

Paul Chidyausiku (1927–)

Zimbabwean poet, novelist and playwright. Chidyausiku began his career as a teacher but then worked as an editor at a publishing company, and of a magazine and a weekly newspaper. He has written many works in his native language Shona as well as *Broken Roots* (1984) in English.

Chidyausiku's work deals with the need to remember the exciting cultural and moral traditions of his country, and to explain these traditions to younger people.

12 An excursion

1 Look at the picture above. What is happening in the picture?
Write down your ideas:

- Perhaps there is a sports match of some kind.
- Perhaps ....
- Perhaps ....

Tell another student about your ideas. Do you agree with each other?

2 Look at the picture again. Use a dictionary to help you find:

a barbed-wire fence
floodlights
a crowd
loudspeakers
a band
banners
a small patch of grass
hoardings

3 Read and listen to this poem:

The Rabbit by **Alan Brownjohn**

We are going to see the rabbit.
We are going to see the rabbit.
Which rabbit, people say?
Which rabbit, ask the children?
Which rabbit? 5
The only rabbit,
The only rabbit in England,
Sitting behind a barbed-wire fence
Under the floodlights, neon lights,
Sodium lights, 10
Nibbling grass
On the only patch of grass
In England, in England
(Except the grass by the hoardings
Which doesn't count.) 15
We are going to see the rabbit
And we must be there on time.

First we shall go by escalator,
Then we shall go by underground,
And then we shall go by motorway 20
And then by helicopterway,
And the last ten yards we shall have to go
On foot.

And now we are going
All the way to see the rabbit, 25
We are nearly there,
We are longing to see it,
And so is the crowd
Which is here in thousands
With mounted policemen 30
And big loudspeakers
And bands and banners,
And every one has come a long way.
But soon we shall see it
Sitting and nibbling 35
The blades of grass
On the only patch of grass

In — but something has gone wrong!
Why is everyone so angry,
Why is everyone jostling 40
And slanging and complaining?

The rabbit has gone,
Yes, the rabbit has gone.
He has actually burrowed down into the earth
And made himself a warren, under the earth, 45
Despite all these people.
And what shall we do?
What *can* we do?

It is all a pity, you must be disappointed,
Go home and do something else for today, 50
Go home again, go home for today.
For you cannot hear the rabbit, under the earth,
Remarking rather sadly to himself, by himself,
As he rests in his warren, under the earth:
'It won't be long, they are bound to come, 55
They are bound to come and find me, even here.'

---

4 (a) Were any of your ideas about the drawing in Exercise 1 the same as in the poem? In the poem, why is everyone going to see the rabbit?
(b) When does the poem take place?

5 Can you guess what these words mean? Tick (a) or (b):

(i) *To long to do something* (line 27) means
- (a) to want to do something very much
- (b) to hate doing something

(ii) *To nibble* (line 35) means
- (a) to eat quickly with big bites
- (b) to eat small pieces of food with small bites

(iii) *To jostle* (line 40) means
- (a) to run and to jump
- (b) to push against another person

(iv) *To burrow* (line 44) means
- (a) to move in a particular direction by digging
- (b) to push close to something

(v) *Disappointed* (line 49) means
- (a) cross and angry
- (b) sad because something did not happen as you expected

6 Read and listen to the poem again. Then, in groups, complete the following sentences about the poem:

(a) There is only one rabbit left in England because ....

....

(b) There is only one patch of grass left in England because ....

....

(c) People only have to walk ten yards to see the rabbit because ....

....

(d) The rabbit is sitting behind a barbed-wire fence under lights because ....

....

(e) Before they see the rabbit, people feel ....

....

(f) The crowd is angry because ....

....

(g) The rabbit burrows under the earth because ....

....

7 (a) Note down all the *natural* things in the poem, and all the *man-made* things.

Natural things	MAN-MADE THINGS

Are there more natural things or man-made things in this poem? What effect does this have?

(b) A number of lines in the poem are repeated more than once. Which ones? What is the effect of repeating them?

8 Do you like this poem? If so, why? If not, why not?

9 Divide into groups of four or five. You are going to read *The Rabbit* aloud in your groups. But first, read through the poem carefully together, and mark down which people in your group will read which lines. Here is an example from one group of students:

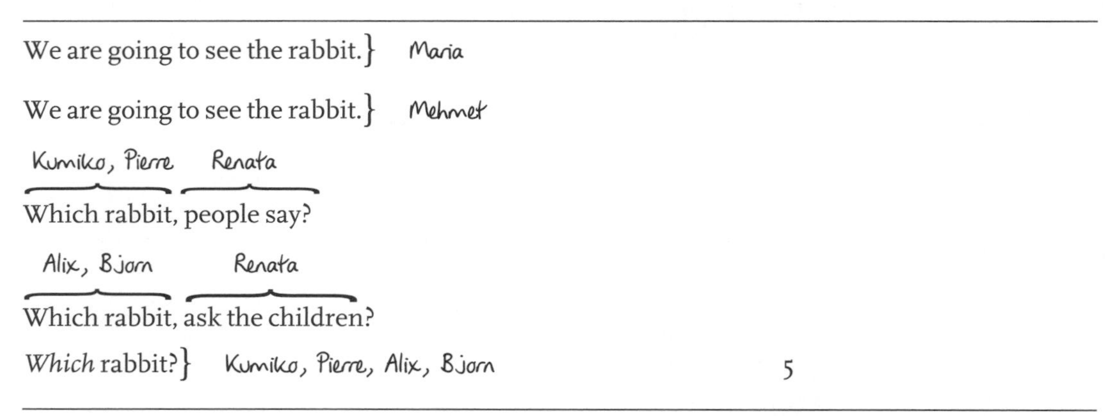
We are going to see the rabbit.} Maria

We are going to see the rabbit.} Mehmet

Kumiko, Pierre — Renata
Which rabbit, people say?

Alix, Bjorn — Renata
Which rabbit, ask the children?

Which rabbit?} Kumiko, Pierre, Alix, Bjorn 5

After you have planned how you will read the poem, practise reading it aloud in your groups. Do this with good pronunciation and lots of feeling! Then perform the poem for the other students in your class.

Creative development

Here are some facts about animals:

White Rhinoceros
(Ceratotherium sumum)

Once many rhinos were found in Africa, south of the Sahara. Hunters have killed thousands because they collect its horns which are sold. There are only 4000 white rhinos left in the world.

Golden Bamboo Lemur
(Hapalemur auerus)

Only discovered in 1989, the Golden Bamboo Lemur is found in the rain forest and one protected area of Madagascar. There are only about 1000 in the world.

Mediterranean Monk Seal
(*Monachus monachus*)

Once many monk seals were found in the Mediterranean and Black Seas and the Atlantic coast of North Africa. Now there are only about 650 left in the world. Many stopped breeding because of tourists on the beaches. Also, new ways of fishing have left them with fewer fish to eat.

How can we protect these animals, so that they do not become like the only rabbit in England? Write down your ideas:

How to protect endangered animals

We should

1 Make laws to stop hunting.

2 ....

3 ....

4 ....

Share your ideas with other students in your class.

Then use your ideas to help you write this poster:

Put your poster on the walls of the classroom for other students to read.

NOTES

Vocabulary

escalator (line 18): a set of moving stairs that carry people up and down between the different levels of a building

the underground (line 19): railway system in which the trains go in passages under the ground; especially the system in London

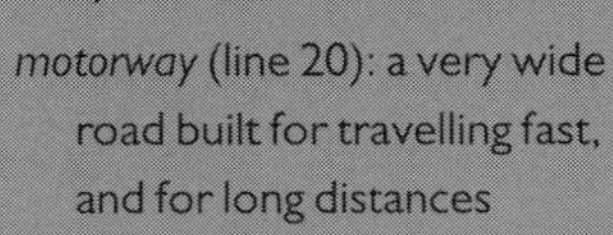

motorway (line 20): a very wide road built for travelling fast, and for long distances

helicopterway (line 21): a word invented by the poet, perhaps to suggest a kind of motorway in the sky for helicopters. A helicopter is a kind of aircraft

mounted policemen (line 30): policemen riding on horses so they can control the crowd better

warren (line 45): underground passages where rabbits live

they are bound to (line 55): they are almost sure to

Alan Brownjohn (1931–)

British poet. Born in London, he taught in various schools and colleges before becoming a full-time writer. He has written many books of poetry, including *Collected Poems* (1988) and *The Observation Car* (1990). He has also written for children (*Brownjohn's Beasts* 1970).

Brownjohn is interested in politics, and has written many poems on social problems. For him, poetry can describe what happens in the world as well as our feelings about it. His poems deal with modern life in a direct and witty way.

KEY

1 Do what I say

3 ... make up their own minds and decide themselves what they want to do.

8 (b) No. Even if you don't drink you can't take your share for your husband. (c) No. Not a towel and a shirt, even if they're old. (d) What's that you said?

9 Poor people must take *what* they can get, and must not hope to *get* exactly what they *want*.

11

	Chivvy	*Feeding the Poor at Christmas*
Some orders in the poem	Speak up Don't stare Don't point Sit up Say please	Bring your plates. Don't move. Don't try turning up for more. Say thank you.
Who gives the order	Grown-ups, e.g. parents and teachers	Rich people who are feeding the poor.
Who the order is for	Children	The poor.

There is an unequal relationship between the person who gives the order, and the person who has to listen. Other examples:
boss and employee, police officer and prisoner, master and servant.

2 Plans and decisions

2 (a) leave school, and go to work at Briar Farm
(b) stay at school, and perhaps go to university to become a teacher
(c) leave school and get a job

3 1 (b) 2 (c) 3 (a) 4 (d)

4 (b) line 5 (c) lines 9–10 (d) lines 13–14 (e) line 15

6 (a) T (b) T (c) F (d) T (e) F

7 The meaning of the words can change depending on how they are said. One possible way is (a) angrily (b) in a resigned way (c) kindly (d) in a determined way

3 Fairy stories

2 witch (c) dragon (b) giant (f) fairy (d) prince (e) princess (a)

3 *objects or things*: glass slipper, gold coin, magic potion, magic wand, poisoned apple, mirror, carriage
places: forest, tower, palace, cave

4 He meets a person or creature (e.g. a witch OR a fairy) who gives him an object that is magic (e.g. a magic potion OR a magic sword). With the magic object, he does something really difficult (e.g. rescues a princess from a giant by making the giant fall asleep OR kills a dragon). He has shown that he is clever OR brave, and so for his reward he marries the princess OR keeps the gold coins in the dragon's cave.

12

The way we usually use the word	*In the poem*
What do we usually 'wrap'? a present, a parcel, a sandwich	lines 14–15: the garden in the sky, the house in the garden
What do we usually 'pack'? a suitcase, a picnic basket, a briefcase	line 16: the garden, the sky and the house in a handkerchief

13 They are used with nouns that we don't usually put them together with. By bringing together things which don't usually go together, new metaphors are created. The effect is to make us think about the deeper meaning of the poem.

4 An empty room

2 Picture 2

5 (A)

CATH Not unless you want to rent it/take it?
OR Not unless you think it's okay/alright?
PHIL Me? No. Not if you don't want to.
CATH No I don't.

(B)

CATH The cooker's a bit old/dirty/grubby.

CATH Yes, it is.

CATH Not very big/clean/nice.

5 *Mystery*

4 (a) 2 (b) 1 (c) 4 (d) 3

5 The people of the town were ~~not~~ surprised. Dom, a ~~brown~~ red-haired boy who lived in the town, wanted to know what Mr Cranley, the ~~doctor~~ butcher, thought about the sunflowers. Mr Cranley ~~and his wife~~ knew Dom's favourite secret, which often made Dom laugh. Dom used to watch people and animals out of his ~~sitting room~~ bedroom window. He imagined that the people were animals, and that the animals behaved like people. For example, he imagined a dog called ~~Rover~~ Bonzo taking his owner for a walk on a lead. Dom told Mr Cranley all about this, and Mr Cranley said that he had a Special Gift. But when Dom asked Mr Cranley if he had a Special Gift, Mr Cranley ~~became very angry.~~ didn't answer

6 Dom follows Mr Cranley as he goes to look at the sunflowers in the snow. Mr Cranley meets some scientists who say there must be a scientific reason for the sunflowers in the snow. Mr Cranley later tells Dom that the flowers will die after Christmas. The next day, more scientists and some journalists come to investigate the sunflowers. In the middle of the night, Mr Cranley disappears and never comes back. Dom tells the scientists that in August he had seen Mr Cranley planting the sunflower seeds. Dom said they grew in the snow because Mr Cranley had a Special Gift. The scientists didn't believe him. After Christmas, the sunflowers died.

10 (i) a (ii) a (iii) b (iv) a (v) b

11 It is strange that
- the matchseller sells matches at the back gate when there is nobody there to buy them.
- the matchseller has been there for weeks, but Edward has never mentioned him.
- Flora never sees him arrive.
- Flora and Edward have never spoken to him.
- Edward has never gone out the back door for two months because of him.

13 The rest of the play is very strange and menacing. Flora invites the matchseller into the house. Both Edward and Flora talk to him separately for a long time, showing their wishes and anxieties. The matchseller does not say a word, and doesn't move. Finally, Flora takes the matchseller to see the garden where she says she will give him lunch. Edward stays inside, and she gives him the matchseller's tray.

6 *Parents*

4 *Verbs describing what the father's hands do*: fix (moth's wing, the thing that makes my doll cry), make (machines, small animals out of clay), mend (the fuse when the world goes dark)
nouns describing things that can hurt or harm the father's hands: blades, anything sharp, bees, nettles, fire, burning oil

5 (a) Many things, such as a broken toy, broken pair of shoes, etc. In the poem, the father fixes a moth's wing – is this to show that he has very gentle hands if he can fix something so delicate?
(b) A room when the lights go off. When the speaker says that 'the world goes dark' does she mean that she becomes very upset and unhappy? The father 'mends the fuse' by comforting and helping her.
(c) Does it mean that the father can fix the lights so that the room isn't dark any more, and the speaker can see the walls of the room? Is the father someone who can mend not just real things (such as lights) but also feelings, by comforting his daughter?
(d) Does she remember her dead mother?
(e) To suggest the quick flow of the speaker's thoughts and feelings.

7 (a) 3 (b) 1 (c) 4 (d) 2

11 (a) The period in history when the speaker's parents, grandparents, etc. were slaves working on sugar plantations in the American South or the Caribbean.

(b) treetalk, windsong, the music of her mother, the leaves whispering, the wind blowing a tune in the grass, her mother's voice. The speaker feels that the sounds are the sounds of her mother, and will stay with her forever. She feels a strong connection with these sounds.

(c) Lines 1–3, line 15 is a kind of repetition of line 3. The repetition creates the effect of a song, since in songs certain parts are often repeated. It also repeats the message - that sugarfields are the speaker's 'home'.

(d) Many ideas are possible here. Does the mother represent the love and strength that black women are able to pass down to their children, even when they were slaves with no power? Does the mother represent 'mother nature' of whom we are all children?

(e) The cultural traditions (particularly the oral tradition of song, poetry, etc.) that black women have passed on to their children even when they were slaves? The beautiful music made by 'mother nature'?

7 *Sharing*

4 (a) push (b) move (c) hit (d) angry (e) surprised (f) nervous

5

Jerry tries to control Peter *physically*
What he does
1 He pokes Peter (lines 6, 1, 16)
2 He punches Peter (lines 21, 24, 26)

Jerry tries to control Peter *with his words*	*What he says*
He shares a secret with Peter	'I'll let you in on what happened at the zoo' (line 1)
He orders Peter to do things	'move over' (lines 7, 11, 16) 'Get off this bench' (line 36) 'Go lie on the ground' (line 43)
He shouts at Peter	'Move over' (line 21)
He makes Peter give him attention	'Listen to me ...'! (line 30)
He behaves as if Peter is a child	'... if you're good I'll tell you the rest of the story' (line 31)
He repeats what he wants a few times	'I want this bench' (lines 30, 36, 38)
He describes Peter in a rude way	'Imbecile! You're slow-witted' (line 41) 'You're a vegetable' (line 43)

6 In the beginning, Peter is friendly and patient, and moves up when Jerry tells him to move up. But then he becomes annoyed and surprised and tries to understand why Jerry is behaving so violently. He says he won't get off the bench, as he sits on it every Sunday and that Jerry can't have everything he wants. He tells Jerry to stop it.

8 (c) Perhaps the characters in the play are compared to animals in a zoo? They are trapped, and may become violent.

Creative development

There is a long argument about the bench. At the end, Jerry pulls a knife on Peter, but then drops it to the ground. Peter picks it up and holds it out to defend himself. Jerry rushes at the knife and kills himself. Peter runs away.

8 *Memories*

9 (a) The effect is to make the dark seem as real and as powerful as a person, rather than a physical quality. Other examples of personification in the poem are '...the black dreams came' (line 10), '...silent terror cried' (line 19), the '...chilly sun saw' (lines 22–3)

(b) The effect is to suggest the emotional coldness of what he experienced. Even the sun, usually connected with light and warmth, here becomes cold. Another example of paradox: 'My *silent* terror *cried*' (line 19).

9 *Maids and madams*

4 1 (e) 2 (a) 3 (f) 4 (d) 5 (b) 6 (c) 7 (g) 8 (h)

5 (a) F (b) F (c) T (d) F (e) T (f) T (g) F (h) F (i) F (j) F

10 (a) She felt very tired from it, and didn't like it.
(b) She said that she loved her.
(c) She didn't love her; did she feel angry with her?
(d) 'The Madam' is Alberta K. Johnson, the maid, and 'her madam' is the woman she works for.
(e) mean/clean, too/through, around if pronounced 'aroun'/down, be/me, no/so, true/you. The rhyme and rhythm of the poem make it seem like a song, but a song with a strong ending!

10 *Music and birdsong*

4 (a) swamp (full of red water) (b) creek (c) gullies (the speaker walked *down* and *up* them) (d) snow grass, speargrass, flax, tussock, manuka, pine tree
(e) to go down (suddenly) and to go up

5
- The speaker asked the blackbirds what they were singing.
- The first time they didn't answer her directly, but said they had to go on singing.
- The second time they stopped singing.

6 (a) She listened very carefully, and with all her concentration.
(b) For the sentence to make sense the first word 'by' should really be followed by the name of a writer or a poet, rather than 'music'. Using the word 'by' three times suggests that the words and music are worked on by humans a lot.
(c) It does not have usual punctuation (e.g. So I said, 'What is the name of the song? Tell me and I will write it, and you can listen at my window when I get the finest musicians in the country to play it, and you will feel so nice to hear your song. So, tell me the name.') It contrasts with the sentence that follows which is very short. This makes clear that the excited flow of the speaker's thoughts in the long sentence is stopped dramatically by the sentence that follows.
(d) Because the birds did not want her to write down their music, to make it organised and controlled like human music? Perhaps 'it was dark' means that the speaker was very sad and upset about this?

7 The words and music of people are made with practice, hard work and planning, and can be given a name. But the music of blackbirds, which cannot be given a name, is natural and sung without plan, work or organisation.

11 *Growing older*

2 old woman called MAUD, her daughter-in-law called HELEN, her son called FRANK

3 (a) talk (b) take (c) think

4 (c)

5

A

Maud Maud
HELEN She said she had a visitor today.

Maud
FRANK Really? Who was that Mother? Who?

Maud Maud
HELEN She isn't listening. Her eyes go all funny when
Maud she isn't listening.

Frank and Helen call Maud 'she' because they think that she doesn't really understand what they are saying. Or does this just show that they are treating her like a child, and don't really respect her?

B

Helen
MAUD Did you make it mother?

Because she is confused, or she is pretending to be confused?

C

the cat the cat
MAUD It makes her really angry if you give her Kit-e-kat. Tell her. Helen
FRANK Who?

Helen Helen
MAUD Your wife. Tell your wife not to waste money on that stuff.

Does Maud talk to Frank about 'his wife' because she is confused, or because she really doesn't like Helen, and refuses to speak to her directly? Is this also a way of saying that the relationship between herself and her son is more important than the relationship between Frank and Helen?

6 (a) That she has been thinking about God, even if she talks about God in a humorous way?
(b) That she feels confused, or is trying to make Helen and Frank think that she is confused.
(c) That she is worried about what will happen to her cat, but perhaps that she is also worried about what will happen to herself.
(d) That she doesn't really care about anything any more, as she will die soon?

10 Younger people.

11

What the grandpa did/does	*What 'they' do*
He walked forty miles a night.	They can't walk a mile.
He never sneezed when his sockless feet got wet.	They catch a cold if their socks get wet.
He sleeps like a baby on a piece of wood.	They can't sleep without a sleeping pill, on a soft mattress.

12 An excursion

4 (a) Because it is the last rabbit in England. (b) The poem is written as if it is taking place now (see the present and future tenses in the poem), but perhaps it suggests a future in which there are no rabbits left.

5 (i) a (ii) b (iii) b (iv) a (v) b

7 (a) *Natural things:* the rabbit, grass, horses (of the police), warren, earth. *Man-made things:* a barbed wire fence, floodlights, neon and sodium lights, hoardings, escalator, underground, motorway, helicopter, loudspeakers, banners.
There are many more man-made things. This suggests a world in which nature has been destroyed by buildings and machines. (b) Many lines are repeated, including 'We are going to see the rabbit' (lines 1, 2, 16) 'the only rabbit' (lines 6 and 7), 'The rabbit has gone' (lines 42 and 43). The effect is to suggest a crowd in which people are talking and chattering. There is a feeling of being excited, which changes to disappointment. The rabbit's words 'they are bound to come' (lines 55 and 56) suggest that it can never be free of people.

Thanks and acknowledgements

The author would like to thank the following for their contributions to *A Window on Literature*:

At Cambridge University Press I would like to thank the following for all their hard work and support: Peter Donovan for getting the whole project off the ground; Isabel Ford for organising the piloting of the material; and, especially, James Dingle for his expert management of the project at all stages.

Many thanks to Ruth Gairns and Joanne Collie for their perceptive comments on an earlier draft of the book, and to Alan Finch for his meticulous editing. I am grateful to the teachers and students in Germany, Japan, Sweden, Brazil, Italy, Turkey, Switzerland and the United Kingdom who tried out the material and made useful suggestions for improving it.

Many thanks, too, to my family for their support.

Many different books and articles have shaped the design of the materials in the book, but I would particularly like to acknowledge the influence of H.G. Widdowson's *Stylistics and the Teaching of Literature* (Longman, 1975) which set me on my path; and Joanne Collie and Stephen Slater's *Literature in the Language Classroom* (Cambridge University Press, 1987), some of whose ideas for activities I have used in this book.

The author and publishers would like to thank the following individuals for their help in commenting on the material and for the invaluable feedback which they provided:

Cristina Lima, Instituto Cultural de Idiomas, Caxias do Sul, Brazil; Mechthild Hesse, Philipp Reis Schüle, Friedrichsdorf, Germany; Harald Weisshaar and Doris Dorsch, Hohenlohe Gymnasium, Öhringen, Germany; Vanna Murri, Bologna, Italy; Vincent Broderick, Kwansei Gakuin University, Nishinomiya, Japan; EwaLisa Carlstrand-Skoog, Kristinebergskolan, Åmål, Sweden; Engin Şen, Gağribey Anatolian High School, Ankara, Turkey; Steven Ebutt, The New School of English, Cambridge, UK; Derek Holmes, Studio School, Cambridge, UK.

The author and publishers are grateful to the following copyright owners for permission to reproduce copyright material. Every endeavour has been made to contact copyright owners and apologies are expressed for any omissions. In such cases the publishers would welcome information from copyright owners.

Michael Rosen, 1979, *Chivvy* on p. 2 from *You Tell Me* by M. Rosen and R. McGough, Kestrel Books. Copyright © Michael Rosen. Reproduced by permission of Penguin Books Ltd.; Eunice de Souza, 1988, *Feeding the Poor at Christmas* on p. 4 from *Black Poetry*, Blackie; C.P. Taylor, *To be a Farmer's Boy* on pp. 9 and 10 from *North: Six Plays by C.P. Taylor*, Methuen. Copyright © The Estate of C.P. Taylor by permission of Alan Brodie Representation Ltd. 211, Piccadilly, London W1V 9LD; Stevie Smith, 1972, *Fairy Story* on p. 15 from *Collected Poems of Stevie Smith*, Penguin 20th Century Classics. Copyright © 1972 by Stevie Smith. Copyright © 1975 James MacGibbon. Reprinted by permission of New Directions Publishing Corp.; Miroslav Holub, *Fairy Tale* on p. 17 from *Notes of a Clay Pigeon*, Secker and Warburg. Reproduced by permission of Random House UK Ltd.; Michael Frayn, 1993, *Here* on pp. 22 and 23, Methuen. Reproduced by permission of Random House UK Ltd.; William Trevor, 1968, *The Sunflowers in the Snow* on p. 28 from *Allsorts 1*, Macmillan Publishers Ltd.; Harold Pinter, 1961, *A Slight Ache* on pp. 30 and 31 from *Plays: One*, Methuen. Reproduced by permission of Faber and Faber Ltd. Copyright © 1961, 1966, 1968 by Harold Pinter. Used by permission of Grove/Atlantic, Inc.; Jeni Couzyn, *My Father's Hands* on p. 36 from Jeni Couzyn: *Life by Drowning: Selected Poems*, Bloodaxe Books, 1985; Barbara Mahone, *sugarfields* on p. 39 from *The Poetry of Black America*, Harper and Row Publishers Inc.; Edward Albee, 1961, *The Zoo Story* on pp. 43 and 44 from *The Zoo Story and Other Plays*, Jonathan Cape. Copyright © 1959, renewed 1987 by Edward Albee. Reproduced by permission of Random House UK Ltd. and by permission of William Morris Agency, Inc. on behalf of the Author; Louis MacNeice, *Autobiography* on pp. 49 and 50 from *Collected Poems* by Louis MacNeice, Faber and Faber Ltd.; Katherine Mansfield, *The Lady's Maid* on p. 55 from *Collected Stories*, Constable and Co. Ltd. 1984, first published 1945; Langston Hughes, 1959, *Madam and Her Madam* on p. 58 from *Collected Poems* by Langston Hughes, Vintage US. Copyright © 1994 by the Estate of Langston Hughes. Reprinted by permission of Alfred A Knopf Inc.; Janet Frame, *The Birds Began to Sing* on p. 63 from *The Lagoon and Other Stories*. Reproduced with permission of Curtis Brown Ltd., London, on behalf of Janet Frame. Copyright © Janet Frame 1951; Jennifer Johnston, 1988, *The Porch* on pp. 68 and 69 from *The Nightingale Not the Lark*. Dublin: Raven Arts Press; Paul Chidyausiku, *A Proud Old Man* on p. 72 from *African Voices*, H. Sergeant (Ed.), Evans Brothers Ltd.; Alan Brownjohn, 1961, *The Rabbit* on pp. 77 and 78 from *The Railings*, Digby Press. © Alan Brownjohn 1983, 1988.

The author and publishers are grateful to the following illustrators, photographers, and photographic sources:

Illustrators: Ann Baun: pp. 12, 14, 27; Kay Dixey: p. 57; Gecko DTP: pp. 16, 50, 51, 86; Paul Hampson: p. 1; Jamie Sneddon: pp. 53, 79; Peter Visscher: pp. 7, 20, 21, 26, 29, 34, 37, 41, 48, 60, 65, 66, 74, 75, 76, 82; Kath Walker: pp. 6, 33.

Photographic sources: John Birdsall Photography: pp. 35 *tr*, 67 *bl*; Birmingham Leisure and Community Services, Libraries and Learning and also the Sir Barry Jackson Trust: p. 42; Konrad Wothe/ Bruce Coleman: p. 80 *m*; Collections/Brian Shuel: p. 67 *tr*; Mary Evans Picture Library: p. 54 *l* and *r*; Brenda Prince/Format: pp. 68 *m*, 71 *m*; Getty Images: p. 38 *b*; Sally and Richard Greenhill: p. 35 *br*; Robert Harding Picture Library: pp. 35 *l*, 68 *l*, 71 *l*; Frank Lane Picture Agency: pp. 80 *l* (Gerard Laci), 80 *r* (F. Di. Domenico/Panda); Pictor International: p. 62; Popperfoto: p. 8 *l*; PowerStock/Zefa: p. 67 *br*; Rural History Centre, University of Reading: p. 8 *r*; Topham Picturepoint: p. 38 *t*; Janine Wiedel: pp. 67 *tl*, 68 *r*, 71 *r*.

t = top *m* = middle *b* = bottom *r* = right *l* = left

Picture Research by Sandie Huskinson-Rolfe of PHOTOSEEKERS.

Cover illustration by Rosalind Hudson.

Design, production and reproduction handled by Gecko Limited, Bicester, Oxon.

Sound recordings by Martin Williamson, Prolingua Productions at Studio AVP.

Freelance editorial work by Alan Finch.

Permissions clearance by Frances Amrani.